Opposing Viewpoints®

America's Youth

Opposing Viewpoints®

America's Youth

Other Books of Related Interest

Opposing Viewpoints®

America's Youth

Roman Espejo, *Book Editor*

Daniel Leone, *President*
Bonnie Szumski, *Publisher*
Scott Barbour, *Managing Editor*

OPPOSING
VIEWPOINTS®
SERIES

GREENHAVEN
PRESS®

THOMSON
────────✳────────™
GALE

San Diego • Detroit • New York • San Francisco • Cleveland
New Haven, Conn. • Waterville, Maine • London • Munich

THOMSON
✳ ™
GALE

LIBRARY OF CONGRESS CATALOGING-IN-PUBLICATION DATA

America's youth : opposing viewpoints / Roman Espejo, book editor.
  p. cm. — (Opposing viewpoints series)
Includes bibliographical references and index.
ISBN 0-7377-1218-X (lib. bdg. : alk. paper) —
ISBN 0-7377-1217-1 (pbk. : alk. paper)
  1. Youth—United States—Social conditions. 2. Youth—United States—Attitudes. I. Espejo, Roman, 1977– . II. Opposing viewpoints series (Unnumbered)
HQ796 .A6818 2003
305.235'0973—dc21
                                       2002021477

| "Congress shall make
no law. . . abridging the
freedom of speech, or of
the press."

First Amendment to the U.S. Constitution

The basic foundation of our democracy is the First
Amendment guarantee of freedom of expression.
The Opposing Viewpoints Series is dedicated to the
concept of this basic freedom and the idea that it is
more important to practice it than to enshrine it.

Contents

Why Consider Opposing Viewpoints?

"The only way in which a human being can make some approach to knowing the whole of a subject is by hearing what can be said about it by persons of every variety of opinion and studying all modes in which it can be looked at by every character of mind. No wise man ever acquired his wisdom in any mode but this."

John Stuart Mill

In our media-intensive culture it is not difficult to find differing opinions. Thousands of newspapers and magazines and dozens of radio and television talk shows resound with differing points of view. The difficulty lies in deciding which opinion to agree with and which "experts" seem the most credible. The more inundated we become with differing opinions and claims, the more essential it is to hone critical reading and thinking skills to evaluate these ideas. Opposing Viewpoints books address this problem directly by presenting stimulating debates that can be used to enhance and teach these skills. The varied opinions contained in each book examine many different aspects of a single issue. While examining these conveniently edited opposing views, readers can develop critical thinking skills such as the ability to compare and contrast authors' credibility, facts, argumentation styles, use of persuasive techniques, and other stylistic tools. In short, the Opposing Viewpoints Series is an ideal way to attain the higher-level thinking and reading skills so essential in a culture of diverse and contradictory opinions.

In addition to providing a tool for critical thinking, Opposing Viewpoints books challenge readers to question their own strongly held opinions and assumptions. Most people form their opinions on the basis of upbringing, peer pressure, and personal, cultural, or professional bias. By reading carefully balanced opposing views, readers must directly confront new ideas as well as the opinions of those with whom they disagree. This is not to simplistically argue that everyone who reads opposing views will—or should—change his or her opinion. Instead, the series enhances readers' understanding of their own views by encouraging confrontation with opposing ideas. Careful examination of others' views can lead to the readers' understanding of the logical inconsistencies in their own opinions, perspective on why they hold an opinion, and the consideration of the possibility that their opinion requires further evaluation.

Evaluating Other Opinions

To ensure that this type of examination occurs, Opposing Viewpoints books present all types of opinions. Prominent spokespeople on different sides of each issue as well as well-known professionals from many disciplines challenge the reader. An additional goal of the series is to provide a forum for other, less known, or even unpopular viewpoints. The opinion of an ordinary person who has had to make the decision to cut off life support from a terminally ill relative, for example, may be just as valuable and provide just as much insight as a medical ethicist's professional opinion. The editors have two additional purposes in including these less known views. One, the editors encourage readers to respect others' opinions—even when not enhanced by professional credibility. It is only by reading or listening to and objectively evaluating others' ideas that one can determine whether they are worthy of consideration. Two, the inclusion of such viewpoints encourages the important critical thinking skill of objectively evaluating an author's credentials and bias. This evaluation will illuminate an author's reasons for taking a particular stance on an issue and will aid in readers' evaluation of the author's ideas.

It is our hope that these books will give readers a deeper understanding of the issues debated and an appreciation of the complexity of even seemingly simple issues when good and honest people disagree. This awareness is particularly important in a democratic society such as ours in which people enter into public debate to determine the common good. Those with whom one disagrees should not be regarded as enemies but rather as people whose views deserve careful examination and may shed light on one's own.

Thomas Jefferson once said that "difference of opinion leads to inquiry, and inquiry to truth." Jefferson, a broadly educated man, argued that "if a nation expects to be ignorant and free . . . it expects what never was and never will be." As individuals and as a nation, it is imperative that we consider the opinions of others and examine them with skill and discernment. The Opposing Viewpoints Series is intended to help readers achieve this goal.

David L. Bender and Bruno Leone,
Founders

Greenhaven Press anthologies primarily consist of previously published material taken from a variety of sources, including periodicals, books, scholarly journals, newspapers, government documents, and position papers from private and public organizations. These original sources are often edited for length and to ensure their accessibility for a young adult audience. The anthology editors also change the original titles of these works in order to clearly present the main thesis of each viewpoint and to explicitly indicate the opinion presented in the viewpoint. These alterations are made in consideration of both the reading and comprehension levels of a young adult audience. Every effort is made to ensure that Greenhaven Press accurately reflects the original intent of the authors included in this anthology.

Introduction

"As social groups, cliques introduce young people to
negative aspects of society, such as conflict and prejudice."
—Debra J. Jordan

"Cliques are not an entirely negative aspect of the high
school social structure."

—Nathan Black

"When kids are tossed together everyday, six hours a day for the entire school year," says psychologist Thomas J. Berdnt, "friendship groupings form quite naturally." These "friend-ship groupings," better known as cliques, are small, tightly knit, autonomous, and sometimes inclusive groups of people that share the same interests or characteristics. Members of cliques often share the same values and exhibit the same be-havior. Although they have been known to form in elemen-tary school, cliques are commonly associated with middle and high school students. In a recent nationwide survey of teenage girls' views of cliques, 96.3 percent of the respon-dents claimed that cliques existed in their schools. In addi-tion, 84.2 percent of the respondents reported that most of their classmates belonged to cliques.

Cliques "can be based on appearance, athletic ability, aca-demic achievement, social or economic status, talent, ability to attract the opposite sex, or seeming sophistication," ac-cording to adolescent development experts Anita Gurian and Alice Pope. The prominent characteristic of a clique usually becomes the clique's label. For instance, a group of self-assured, varsity-jacketed male students might be known as "jocks" while another group's unkempt appearance and spacey demeanor could earn them the "stoner" or "druggie" label. While every high school in America seems to have its own "jocks," "stoners," or "druggies," cliques can become well defined and evolve based on a school's particular envi-ronment and culture. According to journalist Jerry Adler, "At Glenbrook South High School, in the Chicago suburb of Glenview, the [school's peer] groups even take their names from their perches: the fashionable 'wall' people who favor a bench along the wall outside the cafeteria, and the punkish 'trophy-case' kids who sit on the floor under a display of memorabilia."

There are strong incentives for adolescents to join cliques. For example, teenagers use cliques to ease their way through large peer groups. Psychiatry professor Mitch Prinstein claims that cliques are a "sort of shortcut for adolescents to develop friendships and romantic relationships." Prinstein explains that teenagers use cliques to categorize their peers, especially when they move on to middle or high school, where student populations can reach the thousands. Cliques and peer groups also help adolescents establish an identity. Youth expert Alison Landau suggests that "one's peer group helps adolescents to establish an identity, however unstable it may be, apart from their parents. Peer group involvement helps to build confidence among members in their collective and individual abilities to influence their own environment." Most importantly, teenagers join cliques to gain a sense of belonging. "That children identify themselves with a group is part of deciding who they are and having a feeling of belonging," asserts child psychologist Linda Madison.

The cliquishness among students in American high schools has been treated as a normal and relatively harmless youth phenomenon. However, the perception that domineering high school cliques can worsen many students' feelings of depression, alienation, and rage emerged strongly after the Columbine High School shooting in Littleton, Colorado. On April 20, 1999, seniors Eric Harris and Dylan Klebold shot and killed twelve students, a teacher, and wounded twenty-three others before they turned the guns on themselves. The two students were part of the Trench Coat Mafia, a clique of Columbine students that did not mesh well with the rest of Columbine's student body. The Trench Coat Mafia's penchant for black clothing, fingernail polish and makeup, industrial rock music, and alleged involvement with Nazism, satanism, and homosexuality elicited criticism from their peer groups. According to Ben Oakley, who was a sophomore and an athlete at Columbine when the shootings occurred, "[Harris and Klebold] were in the Trench Coat Mafia, and that's something around our school that we considered freaks." Oakley explained that "nobody really liked them. . . . So everyone would make fun of them." Others claimed that jocks bombarded the members of the Trench Coat Mafia with homophobic remarks.

Some commentators believe that Harris and Klebold were exacting revenge on the cliques that taunted them. For example, when the two boys ambushed the school library, they ordered all the jocks to stand up. Also, nearly a year before the shootings, Harris and Klebold had presented a homemade video to a class that depicted two gunmen in trench coats shooting jocks at random in a school hall. Some Columbine students claim that the tragedy was not a surprise because rivalries between cliques at the school had reached worrisome levels. "With all the animosity between the various social groups at Columbine," said Eric Quintana, a former Columbine student and athlete, "something like this was bound to happen."

Other school incidents give further credence to the idea that cliques can incite American teenagers to violence. In March 2001, a New Jersey honor student was arrested for allegedly planning to gun down members of a clique during a wood shop class. In November of the same year, five Massachusetts students were arrested for allegedly plotting to bomb their high school, shoot "jocks, preps, thugs, and faculty," and kill each other before being apprehended by the police.

The Columbine tragedy and the recent spate of school shootings have generated much criticism of high school cliques. Some commentators suggest that cliques can be socially counterproductive because they create hierarchies that alienate some teenagers. For example, violence prevention consultant Jay Bass states that "the downside [of cliques] is that there are some groups that are valued more highly than others . . . those who cannot latch [onto] groups are somewhat disenfranchised." Other commentators insist that cliques thrive at the emotional cost of other students. Aaron R. Kipnis, author of *Angry Young Men: How Parents, Teachers, and Counselors Can Help Bad Boys Become Good Men*, claims that "one of the ways cliques reinforce themselves is by putting down whoever isn't in with them with teasing, taunting, and . . . physical abuse." Some critics even warn that adolescents who are persecuted or rejected by popular or mainstream cliques may react and form cliques that defy the entire school, such as the Trench Coat Mafia. Psychoanalyst Leon Hoffman asserts that "all kids need to belong, and if they can't belong in a positive way at school, they'll find a way to belong to a marginal group like a cult or gang."

However, other analysts maintain that cliques do not create a competitive or hostile school environment. Journalist Jerry Adler claims that the "diversity of cliques has made student life more democratic." Others claim that most cliques are not exclusive and create a sense of belonging for their members. According to student Kerisha Harris, "Too many people think of cliques and immediately conjure up images of a social circle that's as secure as Fort Knox, where only the most beautiful, rich and popular kids can be included. . . . I believe that today's teens are forming cliques not for the purpose of exclusivity, but to find other kids who they can connect with." Additionally, some believe that cliques may prepare adolescents for the complex social structures of the real world. Adolescent psychiatrist David Zinn contends that cliques teach teenagers how to socialize in a society that is "dominated by hierarchies."

The role of cliques in school violence was one of many issues raised in the aftermath of the Columbine tragedy. The transgressive elements of popular culture and entertainment, gun control, and bullying have also been examined in light of school shootings and remain sources of debate. *America's Youth: Opposing Viewpoints* examines these and other issues that face American teens in the following chapters: What Influences America's Youth? What Problems Confront America's Youth? What Values Do Young People Hold? How Can Society Help America's Youth? The authors' views on these issues reflect the difficulty of understanding America's teenagers and devising ways to help them succeed.

CHAPTER 1

What Influences
America's Youth?

Chapter Preface

Many parents believe that television has a detrimental impact on youths. According to a 1999 survey conducted by the Annenherg Public Policy Center, well over 70 percent of parents believe that watching television decreases the time youths spend reading, imparts youths with materialistic values, and arouses youths' interest in sex. The majority of parents also report that television "adds to the loss of child innocence."

Perhaps parents have compelling reasons to fear the influence of television on youths. One study claims that the average youth sees one thousand murders, rapes, and assaults on television every year. In addition, another study reports that 57 percent of all television programs contain violence, while 67 percent of these programs portray violence as humorous. As a result, some analysts suggest that youths, especially younger children, experience "re-entry syndrome" shortly after watching television, which causes them to be more prone to irritability or aggression for a period of time.

Despite these startling findings, some studies note that parents generally do not make an effort to monitor the content or curb the amount of time their children watch television. According to the "National TV Violence Study," 54 percent of youths have television sets in their own bedrooms, and 55 percent of children watch television without their families. Furthermore, Mark Dolliver, editor-at-large at the media-focused periodical *Adweek*, insists that "there's a gap between the percentage of parents who say they issue rules [about television] and the percentage of kids who acknowledge receiving them." Referring to the Annenherg survey, Dolliver alleges that 71 percent of the mothers of sixth- and ninth-graders report that they set television-viewing time limits for their children, while only 35 percent of that age group states that such rules are enforced by their parents.

While many parents believe that television has a negative impact on their children, television is by no means the only influence in young peoples' lives that parents and experts worry about. In the following chapter, the authors debate how other influences such as popular culture, peer pressure, and parents affect the attitudes and behavior of youths today.

"For most [youths] popular culture works as a coarsener, desensitizer, and dehumanizer."

Popular Culture Negatively Influences America's Youth

William J. Bennett

In the following viewpoint taken from testimony given before the U.S. Senate, William J. Bennett argues that the glamorization of violent, antisocial behavior in popular culture is a negative influence on youths. He claims that gratuitous images of brutality in films, television, and popular music desensitize young audiences and encourage some youths to use violence to solve their problems. He insists that the entertainment industry take responsibility for its role in shaping popular culture by regulating the content of films, music, and other products marketed to youths. Bennett is former U.S. Secretary of Education and codirector of Empower America, a policy organization aimed at social and economic reform.

As you read, consider the following questions:
1. According to Bennett, what violent acts take place in *Scream*?
2. How does Socrates describe music's influence on people?
3. How does the author counter the claim that firearms increase violence and crime?

Excerpted from William J. Bennett's statement delivered before the Senate Committee on Commerce, May 4, 1999.

[I] want to commend an article in [the *New Republic*] by Greg Easterbrook.

Here are the first two paragraphs of the article, which talk about the 1996 slasher/so-called "ironic-comedy" movie, *Scream*. The movie was produced by Disney's Miramax division. Easterbrook writes:

Is Mass Murder Fun?

Millions of teens have seen the 1996 movie *Scream*, a box-office and home-rental hit. Critics adored the film. The *Washington Post* declared that it "deftly mixes irony, self-reference, and social wry commentary." The *Los Angeles Times* hailed it as "a bravura, provocative send-up." *Scream* opens with a scene in which a teenage girl is forced to watch her jock boyfriend tortured and then disemboweled by two fellow students who, it will eventually be learned, want revenge on anyone from high school who crossed them. After jock boy's stomach is shown cut open and he dies screaming, the killers stab and torture the girl, then cut her throat and hang her body from a tree so that Mom can discover it when she drives up. A dozen students and teachers are graphically butchered in the film, while the characters make running jokes about murder. At one point, a boy tells a big-breasted friend she'd better be careful because the stacked girls always get it in horror films. In the next scene, she's grabbed, stabbed through the breasts, and murdered. . . . The movie builds to a finale in which one of the killers announces that he and his accomplice started off by murdering strangers but then realized it was a lot more fun to kill their friends.

Mr. Easterbrook goes on to write:

Now that two Colorado high schoolers have murdered twelve classmates and a teacher [on April 20, 1999, at Columbine High School], often, it appears, first taunting their pleading victims, just like celebrity stars do in the movies! Some commentators have dismissed the role of violence in the images shown to the young. . . . But mass murders by the young, once phenomenally rare, are suddenly on the increase. Can it be coincidence that this increase is happening at the same time that Hollywood has begun to market the notion that mass murder is fun?

Mr. Easterbrook's question is a very good one. According to several accounts, Dylan Klebold and Eric Harris enjoyed killing their classmates and teacher. They laughed and hollered, said one survivor, "like it was, like, exciting."

Devotees of Popular Culture

According to media reports, it turns out that Klebold and Harris were fans, even devotees, of a lot in our popular culture. Classmates have said that they listened to, among others, the shock rocker Marilyn Manson, who refers to himself as the "God of F***." Manson recently said that "the end of the world is all we have to look forward to. I'm just pushing the fast-forward button and letting you enjoy the ride." People like Manson do not simply rise by themselves out of America's basements; they are bankrolled by some of America's oldest and most respected corporations. . . .

Consider these words from Marilyn Manson's song "Irresponsible Hate Anthem": "Hey, victim, should I black your eyes again?/Hey, victim,/You were the one who put the stick in my hand/I am the ism, my hate's a prism/Let's just kill everyone and let your God sort them out/F*** it, F*** it, F*** it, F***/Everybody's someone else's nigger . . . /I wasn't born with enough middle fingers." One of the photos on Manson's *Antichrist Superstar* album pictures Manson's genitals hooked up to a hose which drains into the mouths of two men, kneeling, zombie-like, on either side of him. *Antichrist Superstar* . . . rose to Number 3 on the Billboard Album Survey. . . .

This is one of the things [the Senate] should continue to debate: what effect does the popular culture have on the young. In Plato's *Republic*, Socrates said that "musical training is a more potent instrument than any other, because rhythm and harmony find their way into the inward places of the soul, on which they mightily fasten, imparting grace." Rhythm and harmony are still fastening themselves on to children's souls; today, however, much of the music they listen to is imparting mournfulness, darkness, despair, a sense of death.

The events in Littleton were catastrophic for the Columbine students and their families. And it was a horrible moment for this country not just because what happened was so terrible but because it raises questions about key parts of American life. This is a moment that demands hard questions about schools, about parenting, about guns, and about the entertainment industry.

Although [this viewpoint] focuses on the latter, let me say

a word about the gun issue and how it relates to what we are talking about. My view on this is that if somebody is a pro-gun ideologue and says "we can't talk about guns in this issue," they do not have much to contribute to this discussion. Similarly, if some shameless Hollywood ideologue says "we can't talk about the influence of movies or television on this," they do not have much to contribute either. In the matter of the protection of our children, nothing should be off-limits. The issue, obviously, involves a bundle of things. We should talk about all of them.

A Coarsening Effect

Most of us already know that too many of our movies, television shows, music songs, and video games are filled with trash: grisly murder scenes, dismemberment and disembowelment, nonstop profanity, rape and torture scenarios. The relevant questions are: Does it matter and, if it does, how much and what can we do about it?

Anderson. © 2001 by *The Toledo Blade*. Reprinted with permission.

Almost no one, except for a few blinded by financial stakes, thinks that the popular culture is not having a coarsening effect on our kids. The evidence, empirical and anecdotal, is overwhelming. It is clear, abundant, and it is common-sensical. You will hear some of it today.

Now for some kids a small percentage of movies, music, television, the Internet make no difference in their lives; they simply are not affected by the stuff. For most kids, however, the popular culture works as a coarsener, desensitizer, and dehumanizer. That is why most parents, although they are not alarmed or revolting in the streets, are deeply worried. They feel as if they are swimming upstream, fighting against faceless television, movie, and music executives who are fighting against them. This is a very serious problem. We should study it and find out more about it.

But another difficulty is in the very small percentage of kids who are, for all intents and purposes, taken over by the popular culture. Who see the violent movies as a game plan. Who hear the dark, pounding music as a hymn. Who are basically severed and metaphysically separated from their parents, families, and communities. Who begin, as Eric Harris and Dylan Klebold did, to live in a dark parallel universe.

Obviously, this is not simply the work of producers or advertisers. But it may be partly the product of their work. If they believe it is not, then [they] . . . should explain why. As you well know . . . this is something they have been unwilling to do. Recall when the tobacco executives were called to testify before Congress and then bombarded with questions about nicotine and other poisonous additives. That was more than a public hearing; it was a public shaming.

Violence as a "Hook"

The same thing, in my opinion, should happen with the big-shots from Hollywood and Madison Avenue. But here are a few questions [the Senate] might ask them if they do show up:

• Was the scene showing human brains splattered on the car seat a necessary part of your artistic statement? What was the point of including lyrics about child murder and molestation?

• Do you understand the difference between gratuitous violence that simply titillates and violence that serves a purpose in telling a larger story? Can you distinguish between *Casino* and *MacBeth*, between *The Basketball Diaries* and *Braveheart*?

• Who came up with the marketing term "tweens" referring to kids between age eight and 12 and what exactly are you aiming at them? How much money are you spending on targeting young adolescent males?

• Do you use violence as a "hook"? Have you conducted in-depth market research on whether blood and gore appeal to younger audiences? If so, do you need to do this? Can you make your money in a less destructive way? Or is this cultural pollution absolutely necessary? Is this predatory capitalism worthy of your corporation's name?

• Are you at least ashamed when you aim to corner the youth market with images of senseless violence and sex?

To Regulate and Act Responsibly

I will repeat what I have previously said several times before: I am a virtual absolutist on the First Amendment. All of us have a right to make, produce, and sell *almost* anything we want. But the more important question, at least morally and constitutionally, is not so different from the one asked of gun manufacturers. Should you develop, market, promote, and sell something regardless of how degrading or destructive it is?

If we ask the gun manufacturers to regulate themselves responsibly, which we do (and much more), then at least we should ask the entertainment industry to act responsibly (better than trying to regulate them from Washington). We should ask them what they are doing and why they are doing it. Again, I urge [the Senate] to take that action. There are some "gun nuts" in the country, of course; now is an appropriate time to uncover the country's "filth nuts." Some will go on to say that as a percentage of all movies, music, and television, the destructive trash is only a small part. I would respond to this claim by pointing out that the gun folks retort is that only a small percentage of guns are used illegally.

Finally, let me defuse in advance one of my critic's arguments—that we are focusing on the wrong problem when we talk about popular culture since other countries, like Japan, consume the same movies and music that we do but are among the most peaceful nations on earth. Professor Daniel Polsby wrote an article in the *Atlantic Monthly* in which he made the following point: If firearms increase violence and crime, then the rates of violence and crime in Switzerland, New Zealand, and Israel should be higher since their "number of firearms per civilian household is comparable to that in the United States."

The point—and fact—is that we are a complicated country. We are different in many ways from other countries. Our violence is one of those differences. While we are the greatest country in the world, we are also one of its most coarse and most violent. That is not something to celebrate. It is a shame, and needs to be treated that way. By parents, by Congress, and by the entertainment industry.

| *"Odious cultural influences can't be shown to warp [youths]."*

Popular Culture Does Not Negatively Influence America's Youth

Mike Males

Mike Males is a senior researcher for the Justice Policy Institute and author of *Kids and Guns: How Politicians, Experts and the Press Fabricate Fear of Youth*. In the following viewpoint, Males refutes the claim that popular culture—including explicit movies, music, and advertising—spurs youths to engage in dangerous behaviors. For example, he argues that while sales of rap music increased 70 percent between 1990 and 2000, youth violence and crime rates declined. According to Males, politicians, experts, and the press portray popular culture as a negative influence on youths in order to divert attention from the real factors that shape youths' behavior, such as poverty and family dysfunction.

As you read, consider the following questions:

1. What effect did Joe Camel have on teen smoking rates, as stated by Males?
2. According to James Garbarino, how have youths changed in the last twenty-five to thirty years?
3. In Males's view, what section of the youth population experienced increases in homicide and other violent crime rates?

In 1988, R.J. Reynolds introduced its Joe Camel cartoon icon designed to market Camel cigarettes. Everyone from Ralph Nader and anti-tobacco groups to the Centers for Disease Control to conservative tobacco-state lawmakers insisted cigarette ads, especially Joe Camel, lure teens to smoke. Yet, none mentioned the startling fact that in the four years after Joe's advent, every survey showed teenage smoking declined—down 19 percent among high schoolers from 1988 to 1992, twice as fast as the drop among adults.

Further, the biggest decline came among the youngest group (12–13). It wasn't until 1993, when cigarette ad spending fell and market analysts agreed Joe Camel was old hat, that teenage smoking went up.

Surprisingly, over the last 25 years, teen smoking and smoking initiation rates are negatively associated with cigarette advertising and promotion spending—that is, the more companies spend, the less teens smoke, and vice-versa. That fact doesn't fit the needs of the "culture war." Researchers and officials expend strenuous effort (including one dubious study that branded nearly all teens as smokers and denied family and peers have any influence) but have never produced evidence that ads make kids smoke.

Correlation Equals Causation?

Or take the Center for Science in the Public Interests' claim that the marketing of sweet-alcohol beverages, like Budweiser's famous bullfrogs, stimulate teenage drinking. So what? Since these alcohol promos appeared in the early 1990s, high schoolers' drunken driving crashes, binge drinking, and alcohol overdoses plummeted. Under today's simplistic "correlation equals causation" assumption (that is, cultural expression A must be the cause of proximate behavior B), Joe Camel and alcohol ads should be praised for reducing teen smoking and drinking.

But reality doesn't matter to America's raging "culture war," where wild exaggeration and just making things up overwhelm sound social-problem analysis. Leftist warriors sound like their rightist counterparts.

"Teenage women today are engaging in far riskier health behavior than any prior generation," teenage binge drinking "is at record levels," and smoking is "soaring," as ads foment a rebellious "national peer pressure" to defy parents' values, declares progressive media critic Jean Kilbourne (just like right-wing virtuist William Bennett).

"The profound transformation over the last thirty years in the way children look and act . . . seem connected to some of our most troubling and prominent social problems," echoed the conservative Manhattan Institutes Kay Hymowitz, blaming "anticultural forces."

Suburban chronicler Patricia Hersch brands the entire younger generation "an insidious . . . tribe apart." The media's newest youth-violence expert, psychologist James Garbarino, warns the "epidemic . . . of lethal youth violence . . . has spread throughout American society. . . . We have twice as many kids who are seriously troubled as we did 25, 30 years ago and those kids have access to a wide range of dark images, on the Internet, through the videos, video games." Clinicians William Pollack and Mary Bray Pipher label today's youth "lonely, troubled, depressed, confused."

Anecdote and Assertion

What's the evidence for these frightening claims? Little more than anecdote and assertion. In rising panic, culture warriors left to right indict explicit video games, television, gangsta rap music, R-rated movies, Internet images, and "toxic culture" for causing teenage violent crime, drug abuse, sex, and unhealthy behavior. From 1990 to 2000, rap sales soared 70 percent, four million teen and pre-teen boys took up violent video games (as 1992's Nintendo *Mortal Kombat* evolved to 1994's bloody Sega version and sequels), and youth patronage of movie videos and Net sites exploded.

As "toxic culture" dysfluences spread, did *Lord of the Flies* ensue? To the contrary. Perhaps no period in history has witnessed such rapid improvements in adolescent conduct. From 1990 through 1999, teenage violence and other malaise plunged: homicide rates (down 62 percent), rape (down 27 percent), violent crime (down 22 percent), school violence (down 20 percent), property offenses (down 33 percent), births (down 17 percent), abortions (down 15 percent), sexually transmitted diseases (down 50 percent), violent deaths (down 20 percent), suicide (down 16 percent), and drunken driving fatalities (down 35 percent).

Unhealthy youth indexes have fallen to three-decade lows while good ones—school graduation, college enrollment, community volunteerism—are up. Pointedly, the only teenage misbehaviors to increase since 1992, smoking (monthly rates up 13 percent) and drug abuse (overdose deaths up 11 percent, but still low), are the two most subjected to the "culture war's" zero-tolerance interventions. Overall, 80 percent to 90 percent of today's supposedly "depressed, lonely, alienated, confused" younger generation consistently tell surveyors they're happy, self-confident, and like their parents.

These aren't just recent trends; teens as a generation have been improving for several decades. Teenage girls, far from being messed up as Kilbourne and Pipher insist, are far safer today from most major risks (violent death, sexually transmitted disease, pregnancy, homicide arrest, suicide-related deaths, traffic deaths, fatal accidents, drug abuse, heavy drinking, smoking, school dropout, etc.) than girls of 20–30 years ago. Teenage binge drinking has dropped 25 percent since the 1970s, smoking declined 20 percent to 50 percent depending on the measure, and drunken driving deaths are down 40 percent—especially among girls. California, which keeps more precise statistics by race and type of death than other states, records phenomenal declines in teenage suicide, drug abuse, felony crime, and other serious problems over the last 25 years.

Youth Trends and Socioeconomic Disadvantage

The few bad youth trends were related to socioeconomic disadvantage, not culture. The temporary increase in homicide and other violent crime in the late 1980s was not a general youth trend; it was confined to the poorest young men involved in gang conflicts. In 2000, the federal Office of Juvenile Justice and Delinquency Prevention found that law enforcement "policy changes" rather than a real violent crime increase might have sparked more arrests. Contrary to Garbarino and others, murder and other violence by youth is not spreading but becoming more concentrated. Today, America's poorest youths are 40 times more likely to die by homicide and gunfire than the wealthiest, and five-sixths of California's teenage gun deaths occur in just one-tenth of its populated zip codes. While the mega-threats clarioned by the culture war should have killed every American teenager five times over by now, teens today actually display the lowest violent death rate in 50 years!

Aesthetic Taste and Objective Morals

Violent entertainment is not, contrary to the hysterical ravings of anti-entertainment social scientists, anything like tobacco. Tobacco contains uniform chemical substances, the effects of which have been demonstrated in tests over decades on thousands of people. No two pieces of entertainment are the same. Reasonable people do not always agree on what violence is. Many pseudo-scientists who study media, counting "acts of violence," include cartoon and comic violence in their tallies. Philosopher Cornel Hewlett and economist Sylvia Ann West make the outrageous claim that MTV music videos average twenty acts of violence per hour, and that sixty percent of programming on MTV links violence to degrading sexual portrayals. As someone who watches a lot of MTV and who submits music videos to them on a regular basis, I can say unequivocally that these statistics are grossly inaccurate. Because of the scrutiny they are under, MTV has more stringent standards limiting sex and violence than virtually any other entertainment medium. There is virtually nothing on the channel that depicts violence as explicitly as movies, network television, or literature. Sex on MTV is overwhelmingly, conventionally, (and nonviolently) heterosexual and much less graphic than in other media. Aimed at teenagers and people in their early twenties, MTV videos can seem puerile to adults or to intellectual or iconoclastic kids. But it is wrong to confuse subjective aesthetic taste with objective morals.

Danny Goldberg, *Tikkun*, September/October 1998.

None of culture warriors' dire claims of epidemics of depressed, alienated, self-destructive, murderous youth are even remotely verifiable—and younger, pre-teen kids are safer still. No matter. Culture critics aren't concerned with reality, but with sin: blood-spewing video games, bikini-team beer ads, and other repulsive cultural manifestations must be causing damage. Culture warriors' phoniness is revealed by their indifference when real-life killers cite unexpected media triggers: the stalker who shotgunned actress Rebecca Schaeffer worshipped the anthemic Irish band U2, Oklahoma's 15 year-old school shooter idolized the PG movie *Patton*, and numerous mass-killers quote the Bible.

The culture war is not just phony, but reactionary. It commodifies powerless groups to project a fearsome image of constantly escalating menace, suppresses discussion of real social inequalities, and promotes repressive government solutions. Youth are the most convenient population upon which to project damage, keeping the debate safely away from questioning adult values and pleasures that form the real influences on youths. In short, the culture war is not about changing genuine American social ills such as high rates of child poverty, domestic violence, and family disarray, but fomenting an endless series of moral panics that obstruct social change.

Political movements to strip youth rights and institutional youth-fixers have proliferated to profit from fear, generating more scary "studies" proclaiming ever "new," "alarming," and "rising" youth crises that are then recycled by culture warriors as if special-interest self-promotion equaled science. The Carnegie Corporation recasts the healthiest, safest generation of young teens age 10–14 ever as a mass of "grim statistics" and "tragic consequences." (In truth, violent fatality rates among today's younger teens are an astounding 48 percent lower than in the supposedly pastoral 1950s Carnegie extolled). Carnegie deplored the "freedom, autonomy and choice" among teens for unprecedented "threats to their well-being."

Denying Fundamental Responsibility

Healthier Western nations recognize it's normal for an adolescent to experience depression, anger, lust, body image confusion, anxiety, sexy music, cathartic games, evil media messages, corporate pitches, dangerous temptations, free time with peers, consumer interests, all those untoward growing-up influences about which Americas kiddie-savers spread apocalyptic terror. Even if some kids get into trouble, modern remedies like curfews, Prozac, zero-tolerance, and mass lockup only make things worse.

American youth do suffer real threats (as opposed to fictional booze marketing and R-rated movies). Fourteen million kids grow up in abject poverty, 2,000 die and half a million are treated in hospital emergency rooms from domestic violence every year, and 15 million have addicted parents. Americans' preference for indulging self-righteous moral crusades to avoid tough decision-making is a big reason the U.S. remains unable to confront vastly outsized levels of murder, violence, gunplay, unplanned pregnancy, addiction, drunkenness, preventable disease, and other social ills that other industrial nations better control.

Odious cultural influences can't be shown to warp kids, but the culture war itself clearly corrupts grownups to dodge and deny fundamental responsibility.

VIEWPOINT 3

"[Youths] are particularly prone to peer pressure."

Peer Pressure Is an Important Influence on America's Youth

Kathiann M. Kowalski

In the following viewpoint, Kathiann M. Kowalski asserts that peer pressure can have a powerful impact on youths' physical and emotional well-being. Kowalski claims that positive peer pressure may persuade youths to act responsibly, while negative peer pressure may influence youths to behave in ways harmful to themselves and others. She suggests that youths can counter negative peer pressure by defining the consequences of obeying their peers' demands and finding the courage not to be persuaded. Kowalski is a writer of children's books and the author of *Teens Rights: At Home, at School, Online*.

As you read, consider the following questions:

1. How does Kowalski define peer pressure?
2. What theories have been postulated to explain why youths are prone to peer pressure, according to the author?
3. According to Michael Farrell, why does peer pressure make youths highly susceptible to drug and alcohol use?

Excerpted from "How Peer Pressure Can Affect You," by Kathiann M. Kowalski, *Current Health 2*, September 1999. Copyright © 1999 by Weekly Reader Corp. Reprinted with permission.

Erin was a sophomore from Walnut Creek, California, when she found two of her friends in the girls' room with lines of crystalline white powder all laid out. They said the white powder was "crank," a slang term for methamphetamine. "Let me try some," Erin said. That impulsive decision led Erin to a problem with addiction that eventually landed her in drug rehabilitation.

Nick came from a nice family in St. Paul, Minnesota. But that didn't keep him from hanging out with gang members. He said he enjoyed their companionship. When Nick got stabbed, however, being in the gang wasn't fun anymore.

Erin and Nick let themselves become victims of peer pressure.

Peer pressure can be deadly too. In April 1999, at Columbine High School in Littleton, Colorado, Eric Harris and Dylan Klebold, members of the Trench Coat Mafia, killed 12 fellow students, a teacher, and themselves. One possible reason for the rampage was the teasing and taunting they received as part of the Trench Coat Mafia clique—an example of peer pressure at its worst.

A Powerful Force

Peer pressure is the influence that people in your age group (your peers) exert on you. Often, the pressure includes words of encouragement, criticism, or persuasion. Or, it can be unspoken, as when group members sport similar clothes or hairstyles. Either way, peer pressure can have a profound impact on your physical and emotional health.

Why does peer pressure work so well among teens? "I think it works because kids are trying to figure out their place in their school, in their group, or whatever," observes Bernice Humphrey at Girls Incorporated's National Resource Center in Indianapolis, Indiana. "So they try to compare what they do with what other folks are doing." Teens naturally try to avoid negative attention so they won't seem weird, abnormal, or uncool. They want to fit in.

Psychologists differ on why teens are particularly prone to peer pressure. One theory says that it simply feels good to be accepted by a group, and that acceptance satisfies a need to belong. Another theory points out that life becomes easier when we act like others, or conform, rather than be different from others. Still another theory says people tend to view themselves as they think others see them, so they change to conform to others' expectations.

"Whatever the underlying motive, the effect is extremely powerful," says Robert Bornstein, a psychology professor at Miami University in Ohio. "Kids really do care what their peers think, and they really are working very hard to gain acceptance and status within the peer group."

Positive Peer Pressure

Peer pressure doesn't have to be negative. In fact, it can often be a good thing. High school senior Annie says her close friends form a loyal support system. "I know that I can always call them and tell them anything," Annie says.

Peer pressure can encourage good habits. When 14-year-old John Richards' friends play sports in Rocky River, Ohio, he feels encouraged to exercise too. "I got pressured into doing some volunteering," says 18-year-old Ariel Albores from Cleveland, Ohio. He's glad his school group involved him in community service.

Peer pressure can help give you the added strength to avoid risks to your health. Elizabeth Pozydaev, 15, from Fairview Park, Ohio, says no one in her group is into drugs. Most of her friends avoid cigarette smoking too.

Peer pressure can also encourage you to find ways to get along with others. Shouting and screaming don't resolve disputes. To get along with others, you have to know how to speak up for yourself. But you also must become skilled at resolving everyday disagreements in ways that make everyone a winner. Teens who want to keep their friends can benefit from these skills.

Risky Business

Despite the potential for good, peer pressure can have disastrous effects. "The best predictor of a kid using drugs and alcohol is what his or her friends do," says sociologist Michael Farrell at the State University of New York (SUNY) at Buffalo. The people selling drugs for the billion-dollar drug industry aren't TV stereotypes. "They're your classmates," says Farrell, "and the people using and modeling drug use are your classmates." This "in-your-face" factor produces a constant pressure that teens must deal with.

And when alcohol flows freely at parties, the pressure mounts to drink excessively. Binge drinking in college fraternities made national headlines in 1997 and 1998, when students died from alcohol overdoses at the Massachusetts Institute of Technology, Louisiana State University, and Case Western Reserve University.

The Price of Group Membership

Becoming a member of a peer group is one of the primary developmental tasks of adolescence. Peer groups influence adolescent socialization and identity by allowing young persons to explore individual interests and uncertainties while retaining a sense of belonging and continuity within a group of friends. Although a key aspect of normal adolescent development, there may be costs associated with becoming a member of a group of people. [According to sociologists D.R. Clasen and B.B. Brown,] some have considered peer pressure the "price of group membership," which research has linked to a variety of potential problems, including substance abuse, risk-taking behavior and delinquency, as well as dating attitudes and sexual behavior. Belonging to a group requires conformity to group interests and desires, which may not be strictly a matter of individual preference. For many young persons, substance use, risk-taking behavior, and sexual activity may represent efforts to "conform to the norms of the group and to demonstrate commitment and loyalty to other group members" [according to sociologists P.R. Newman and B.M. Newman].

Darcy A. Santor, Deanna Messervey, and Vivek Kusumakar, *Journal of Youth and Adolscence*, April 2000.

Peer pressure can also contribute to criminal behavior. The U.S. Office of Juvenile Justice and Delinquency Prevention estimates that more than 23,000 teenage gangs roam America's cities. Some teen cliques encourage members to shoplift. Gang members are under pressure to take part in the group's violent ways. Otherwise, they risk not only alienation, but bloody retaliation.

Other risky behaviors flow from peer pressure. A study in the medical journal *Pediatrics* found that teens who became sexually active often did so because they thought it increased their status among their peers.

Academic performance also can suffer. High-achieving students hang out together at many schools, which reinforces their desire to do well. But researchers found that many students experience peer pressure to slack off at school.

Then there are potential psychological costs. "People in my neighborhood were always questioning your masculinity, your manhood—mocking you," notes Ariel. He says the rough environment where he lived was "seriously hard-core."

Even "nice" kids can get nasty. More than 70 percent of girls answering a *Teen Magazine* survey said they saw clique members act mean toward outsiders. Forty percent said they personally experienced clique cruelty.

The cliques at Elizabeth's high school include a cool group, a smart group, druggies, jocks, and babes. "There are a few kids who can be really nice if you're alone with them," says Elizabeth, "but if they get with their friends, they are very careful about who they talk to and what they say. They want to be cool with their friends." To avoid being left out, clique members often tolerate or even join in group bullying. In the process, the self-esteem of the kids who give in to the pressure suffers.

When the Pressure's On

To control peer pressure, the first step is to spot it. Temptations, taunts, and threats are three ways teens can pressure each other.

1. The temptation, or "sell," tantalizes you with possible pleasures and thrills. One teen might boast how good he feels when he's high. Another teen may encourage you to come shoplifting because "we won't get caught." Someone else might suggest it would be fun to break into a home or school and destroy property.

2. Taunts include put-downs and sarcasm. "Did your mommy tell you not to drink with us?" "Are you afraid to try it?"

3. Threats of exclusion also exert pressure. "If you want to stay in our group, you'll go along," or the guilt trip: "If you were really my friend, you'd let me copy your answers."

Peer pressure also operates subtly. "The people you hang

around with are going to have a profound impact on you over time," stresses Dr. Farrell. "If they're all smoking, you can say, 'Well, I'm not going to do that.' But that model and that pressure's going to be there all along."

That's what happened when Ashley's friends started smoking marijuana and drinking alcohol. She had always thought of herself as anti-drug. Over time, however, Ashley grew curious. Soon she was getting high with her friends almost every day.

Four D's of Friendly Refusal

How do you handle peer pressure? Knowing what to do about negative peer pressure can help you make good choices. Between 5,000 and 6,000 girls each year go through Girls Incorporated's Friendly PEERsuasion program. In turn, they help other kids learn how to resist negative peer pressure with the program's "Four D's of Friendly Refusal": determine, define, decide, and do.

• "The first 'D' is to determine the risk," says Bernice Humphrey. Is this trip to the mall really a shoplifting excursion? Will there be alcohol at that party? Are kids likely to use drugs when they get together after school?

• Then, define the consequences. "What are the negative things that can happen if you participate in that risky behavior?" asks Humphrey. Understanding the adverse consequences of smoking, drinking alcohol, taking drugs, engaging in risky sexual activity, and breaking the law helps you evaluate the situation. When you weigh adverse consequences against any momentary thrills, chances are you'll decide those are risks you don't want to take.

• Next, decide what you want to do right now. "Hopefully you'll replace that negative alternative with a positive option," says Humphrey. Instead of staying at a party with drinking, for example, you might catch a movie or grab a snack.

• The final "D" is having the courage to do what's best for you. Invite your friends to join you in something better, says Humphrey, but don't let their refusal deter you. If they won't join you, leave immediately.

Sharon Scott, family counselor and author of *How to Say No and Keep Your Friends*, suggests that teens have a range of possible responses beyond simply saying no and leaving the scene. Options include ignoring the offer to do something wrong, making a brief excuse, joking about it, changing the subject, or returning the challenge. If someone argues that a real friend would help him or her cheat on a test, for example, you can counter that real friends don't use pressure to make you do something wrong.

In any case, avoid long arguments. Thirty seconds is plenty of time to say no and repeat it. If other people don't get the message by then, it's their problem, not yours. Walk away.

"If you feel you don't want to do something, just stand up for yourself and say no," says Ariel. "For the most part, people respect you more if you stand up for what you believe in rather than just going along with whatever they want."

"Rely on yourself to know what's right, and don't place too much value on what your friends think," adds 18-year-old Christopher. "Hold your own ideals and values high."

Accentuate the Positive

Even before other teens try to pressure you into risky or illegal behaviors, you can take steps to control the situation. "It really does matter who you choose as your friends," says Dr. Farrell.

"The people you hang out with shape your personality," adds Annie. If you don't want to be exposed to dangerous behaviors, decide for yourself to avoid groups that do those behaviors.

"This is a good time in your life to stand up for yourself and be your own person," says Christopher. "Don't put so much emphasis on acceptance by one particular group. If they don't want to accept you, go and find your own circle of friends."

Following through on that advice is easier if you're involved in volunteer work, sports, clubs, or other activities that help you appreciate your own worth. "We need to make sure that all kids have positive experiences," says Bernice Humphrey at Girls Inc., "where they can feel confident about what they know, who they are, and their skills." These experiences help keep things in perspective when peer pressure turns negative.

Breaking away from any group can be difficult. But remember that you're not alone. A survey by The BrainWaves Group in New York City found that the majority of American teens say they enjoy learning, accept the responsibility of jobs and chores, plan to continue their education, and aim for a good career. Find other teens who model the goals and behaviors you want for yourself. As you share each other's friendship, you'll stay on track for what you really want in life.

"Peer pressure . . . is a myth that enables adults to explain youths' troubling behaviors."

Peer Pressure Is Not an Important Influence on America's Youth

Michael T. Ungar

In the following viewpoint, Michael T. Ungar argues that peer pressure is a myth invented by adults to explain youths' misbehavior. Ungar asserts that contrary to the popular image of powerless teens succumbing to peer pressure, youths intentionally adopt the behavior and appearance of their peers in order to obtain personal and social power. For example, researchers studying at-risk teens found that youths labeled troublemakers may misbehave not because of peer pressure but because they choose to project themselves as "tough" to gain respect. Ungar, a sociologist, conducts research on youths at risk.

As you read, consider the following questions:
1. According to M.L. Pombeni, E. Kirchler, and A. Palmonari, what are some positive peer groups in youths' lives?
2. In the author's view, what is the second stage of youths' development of power?
3. How does Melissa break the gender norms of her peers, according to Ungar?

Excerpted from "The Myth of Peer Pressure," by Michael T. Ungar, *Adolescence*, Spring 2000. Copyright © 2000 by Libra Publishers, Inc. Reprinted with permission.

The construct of peer pressure was examined as part of a larger study investigating the relationship between the process of empowerment and the mental health of high-risk adolescents. It can be defined as pressure from peers to "do something or to keep from doing something else, no matter if you personally want to or not" [according to sociologists D.R. Clasen and B.B. Brown], and has been used to explain young people's behavior. . . .

Myths shape thinking and provide a convenient way to organize thoughts and experiences. While people contribute to the meaning of myths through participation in social discourse, or collective conversation, the decision as to which myths become prominent and how they are interpreted depends on who has the most power in that discourse. It may be adults, not teens, whose description of events is reflected in the term "peer pressure.". . .

Misconduct and the Peer Group

While the relationship between the peer group and misconduct has received considerable attention, the personal agency of individual members has often been ignored. For example, R. Pearl, T. Bryan, and A. Herzog studied urban and suburban youths with and without learning disabilities and their response to peer pressure. They reported that females felt less pressured than did males to engage in misconduct, learning disabled youths were more likely to engage in misconduct, and urban students (mostly from ethnic minority groups) were more likely than their white suburban counterparts to anticipate negative consequences from peers if they refused to engage in misconduct. However, questions arise with regard to why teens choose to associate with peers who are delinquent and why collectively these peer groups choose antisocial behaviors. Do delinquent urban youths from minority cultural groups have as many options to define themselves as powerful and competent as do their white suburban counterparts? Do learning disabled youths find in delinquent acts the personal competence they lack elsewhere in their lives? Why are females more likely to conform to broader social norms?

Other researchers have taken a more optimistic view of

the adolescent peer group. They have found it to be necessary for the accomplishment of developmental tasks and critical for cognitive and emotional growth. M.L. Pombeni, E. Kirchler, and A. Palmonari have indicated that adolescents who highly identify with their peer group "not only are more inclined to ask other people, peers as well as friends, parents and other adults, for support, to accept their offers of support, and to talk about their problems, but they also seem to be more often able to resolve their problems than low-identifiers." They emphasized that "street groups, although commonly perceived as often close to deviant groups, such as drug abusers or delinquent cliques, provide an equally important and helpful juvenile subculture as formal groups committed to sports, religious programs or politics. The crucial factor is getting involved with peers, sharing thoughts and feelings with the group, rather than the nature of the group itself." Attachment to the peer group helps the young person avoid the problem of alienation, even when the identification is with a group of delinquents. In fact, interventions have successfully used the positive aspects of peer relationships to benefit delinquent youth. . . .

Further, other research has shown the presumed negative influence of the peer group to be exaggerated. For example, after a meta-analysis of the literature, K.E. Bauman and S.T. Ennett concluded that peer influence on drug use is overestimated. They argued that the "strong and consistent correlation between drug use by adolescents and the drug use that they attribute to their friends" can be explained by the selection of friends and the projection by adolescents of personal behaviors onto their peers. Bauman and Ennett hypothesized that the causal relationship is the opposite of that implied by the term peer pressure.

L. Michell and P. West investigated the issues of selection and projection in regard to smoking and peer group influences. They found that 12- to 14-year-olds who did not want to smoke "avoided particular social situations and contexts associated with smoking behavior, or chose non-smoking friends, or, if necessary, dropped friends who started to smoke." They concluded: "Data from this study lead us to reject definitions of peer pressure as one-way and coercive, and assumptions about adolescents as socially incompetent and vulnerable. . . . We agree that individual choice and motivation need to be put back on the drug use agenda and that social processes other than peer pressure need to be acknowledged. These may have more to do with the way like-minded young people group together as friends and then cooperatively develop a 'style' which may, or may not, include smoking.". . .

An Important Question

In the course of studying the relationship between the process of empowerment and mental health during adolescence, an important question arose: What role do friends and peer groups play in the lives of teenagers? It was thought that experiences of power in relationships with peers might somehow protect high-risk youth against the impact of biopsychosocial risk factors, such as poverty, the mental illness of one or both parents, physical and sexual abuse, family violence, neglect, intellectual and physical challenges, addictions, and mental disorders (e.g., depression). Some combination of three or more of these risk factors were present in the lives of the participants in this research. . . .

The participants were 41 high-risk adolescents, ages 13 to 18, who had been in therapy within the last 12 months. High risk was determined by the presence of three or more of the previously noted biopsychosocial factors known to jeopardize mental health. The author and at least two other clinicians (with supervisory experience) had to agree that the adolescent showed such characteristics. . . .

Each teen participated in two interviews lasting one to one-and-a-half hours. The first interview included open-ended questions, covering issues related to adolescence, mental health, relationships, competencies, coping strategies, and experiences of power and control. Questions regarding relationships with family, peers, and community included: "Who are the important people who have had an influence in your life, before and now?" "Can you tell me about your relationships with your family? Friends? Other people in your community?" Clinical case files, including family data, were reviewed prior to the interviews to gain a better understanding of participants' histories. . . .

Power and the Peer Group

Peer groups were described by participants as forums in which to enhance personal power through the assertion of both an individual and a collective identity. Laura (age 14) emphasized the tolerance peers show toward each other. Though her parents are convinced otherwise, Laura noted that her individuality is not compromised by her relationships with peers: "I'm my own unique person and nobody is like me and nobody will ever be just like me. I don't like it when people are the same. People should have their own identity and know who they are." She asserted that she chooses who she associates with on the basis of which relationships enhance her sense of self: "I just stay with my friends who like me and believe in the way I do things and don't believe in what everyone else says."

Peer Pressure and Smoking

According to a study published in the *Journal of the National Cancer Institute*, tobacco advertising and promotion influence adolescents' decision to begin smoking significantly more than does peer pressure. While both receptivity to tobacco advertising and exposure to cigarette smokers were correlated with susceptibility to smoking, the relationship was stronger for receptivity to advertising. Specifically, the researchers, led by John Pierce of the University of California at San Diego, discovered that non-smoking adolescents who are receptive to tobacco advertisements are 3.91 times more likely to smoke than teens who do not notice tobacco advertisements. In contrast, adolescents who were exposed to family members and peers who smoked were 1.89 times more susceptible to begin smoking than those who were not exposed to smokers.

Smoking Control Advocacy Research Center, "Studies Correlate Cigarette Advertising with Smoking Initiation Among Youth," November 22, 1995.

When asked specifically about their attire, the adolescents focused on the unique ways they express their sense of self through clothing. Patricia, a streetwise 14-year-old who was well-known in her community as a leader among other troubled teens, appeared to conform to her peer group in dress and behavior. Yet, she spoke extensively about how she differs from her peers: "Everybody knows this about me, that I dress for me—nobody else. . . . Like one day I'll wear nice preppy clothes, then the next I'll wear huge jeans that fall off my butt. Like if I think a big long skirt is neat, and if my friends don't like it, I'll say, 'Don't look at it then.'" Casual observers overlook the subtle differences in this form of personal expression.

Kevin, a 15-year-old "delinquent," saw himself as different from other delinquents because, he said, "I always help my friends out when they have problems, and I give good advice." Stephanie, age 16, who had problems with truancy and violent behavior, insisted she is different from her closest friends because she does not drink, wanting to avoid becoming an alcoholic like her mother and aunts and uncles. In each case, apparent conformity hid the important power these adolescents had within the peer group to be themselves.

Three Developmental Stages of Power

In three stages, adolescents progress toward greater power and self-expression in their interactions with peers, family members, and others in the community. Though these stages are sequential, high-risk teens move back and forth between them as they attempt to cope with the multiple problems they face.

During the first developmental stage, high-risk teens are stuck with one self-definition. Although some choice may be exercised in the selection of this identity, there are few alternatives from which to choose. The peer group helps to reinforce the one label the individual teen controls. These teens typically include the repeat offender whose only talent is getting into trouble, the suicidal youth who has few other coping strategies, and the youth who sacrifices his or her needs for the needs of others.

The second developmental stage is reached when teens become chameleons. They appear to adopt the labels available to them from the different groups of people with whom they interact, including peers. These youths are the ones who do fine in school, but act violently toward themselves or others when at home, or appear confident when in leadership positions, but surprise adults with their lack of self-esteem.

The third developmental stage is achieved when youths experience the control and competence necessary to construct self-definitions of their own choosing, which are accepted by peers, family, and community members. These are resilient, self-assured individuals who steadfastly proclaim to the world, "This is who I am. Accept me." They use the peer group to assert unique aspects of their identity. Although they may be gifted at sports or academics, many act out socially (for example, running away from home as a result of physical or sexual abuse).

The following case histories help illustrate these three stages of development.

Being Stuck

Tommy (age 16) has attempted to cope with his circumstances by finding one powerful self-definition and tenaciously holding on to it.

In the presence of adults, Tommy is quiet, withdrawn. He is a strong, good-looking young man who has been in and out of jail and foster homes throughout his adolescence. Tommy's mother has moved the family many times throughout her son's life. She talked of five different men who were the fathers of her eight children; in some cases, she was not quite certain who was the father of which child. Alcoholism, spousal abuse, and child abuse characterize the history of this family. Of his siblings, Tommy most idealizes his 17-year-old brother, Jason, who is in a provincial jail (serving a one-year sentence for theft and assault). "No one messes with him," Tommy explained. . . .

Given the problems confronting him at home, Tommy's "solution" has been to construct the one powerful identity that is readily available to him: delinquent. In and out of custody, Tommy finds peers who accept him in this one way, and who reflect back to him his status as a troublemaker. Even when Tommy tries to be something other than a delinquent, he remains stuck with this label. Unable to construct another self-definition, he tries to sustain the image of a "tough guy" among his peers: "I want people to think I'm tough.". . .

The Chameleon

In their search for acceptance, high-risk teens may share their power of self-definition with others through superficial conformity. Conformity brings a measure of acceptance within the group, and allows the vulnerable youth to use group identity to appear more powerful than he or she feels otherwise. The chameleon-like coping strategies of Tanya (age 14) are typical. . . .

Tanya has done well in school and has become involved in the politics of her low-income housing project. She is very proud of her recent appointment to the board of the recreation center. She makes a good impression on adults, though she has only a few close friends her own age. She tries desperately to fit in with her peers by adopting their mannerisms, but is seldom accepted as much by them as she is by adults.

Tanya has once been caught shoplifting, having stolen a few cosmetics that she said her family could not afford. Tanya spends most of her time away from home, involved in extracurricular activities.

Tanya's ability to fit in with adults, as well as her constant effort to make new friends with peers, helps her avoid feelings of alienation and depression. She has created a large network of relationships that sustain many different identities, though she asserts little influence, especially with her peers, over the labels she is given in each setting. Tanya explained: "I change when I'm in a particular environment. How I'm talking here is not how I talk anywhere else. I'm a totally different person here than I am with my mom or my dad. I'm never the totally same person in every spot. I don't want people to know me totally, just a little bit about me. Feels better that way."

This changeability is not simply a function of her age and the associated search for identity. Tanya alters who she is with each group of peers and adults she encounters because she lacks influence over how the labels given to her are constructed. Playing the chameleon helps teens like Tanya learn and practice the social skills they need to develop a self-definition of their own choosing. . . .

Acceptance

In the third stage, the high-risk teen shares in the construction of one or more identities. Several of the participants, such as Melissa [age 15], had achieved this level of power. . . .

With her peers, Melissa is outgoing and assertive. She has

a boyfriend, and insists that she maintains a great deal of say over how she expresses her sexuality. She feels comfortable being who she is when out of the home. She also likes to break with the gender norms of her peers, and is very proud of her success in an automotive course.

Melissa's search for a positive self-definition has taken her out of her home, where she is seen as a "substitute mother." Her self-constructed identity within the peer group enhances how she feels about herself. With her peers, she is accepted both as a member of a group and as a unique individual. She stated: "I make all my own choices. Like being with a guy or not, and who my friends are, and if I smoke or if I don't smoke."

Other high-risk teens demonstrated this capacity to exercise control over the labels assigned to them. Johnny, a former addict, organized a Narcotics Anonymous group for young people in his community. He had used his time in custody to create a new identity for himself. Troy recently confronted his abusive father about the emotional and physical abuse he suffered as a child, changed peer groups, and nurtured other friendships. Beth, an ecologically minded young woman, gained self-esteem from participation in social causes. This, in turn, helped her deal with the chaos in her family. These are just a few of the paths high-risk youths have followed in constructing identities that bring them acceptance and power.

Peer Pressure Is a Myth

The concept of peer pressure leads to the belief that the peer group demands conformity to its norms, which may include delinquency. The notion that adolescents experience anxiety or frustration when unable to follow [in the words of Brown] "the dictums of their peers" supports the idea that teens sacrifice personal agency. However, the high-risk youths in the present study provided a different perspective. The peer group was experienced as a forum in which to participate in the collective construction of both a group and individual identity. Arguably, both group and individual status reflect the ability to convince others of self-worth.

By exploiting opportunities available to them through the

peer group, high-risk youths challenge the stigmatizing labels assigned to them by their families and community. As they participate with peers in the creation of self-definitions, they move from feelings of worthlessness and disempowerment to confidence and well-being.

In sum, peer pressure was revealed to be a myth that enables adults to explain youths' troubling behaviors. Rather, the high-risk adolescents in the present study indicated that adoption of the behavior and appearance of peers was a consciously employed strategy to enhance personal and social power.

"There's been a pretty significant myth that [youths'] peer groups are important and parents are not."

Parental Influence Is Important to America's Youth

Susan Gilbert

In the following viewpoint, Susan Gilbert counters the assertion that parental influence is not as significant as peer influence in youths' lives. Gilbert claims that youths who are close to their parents are less likely to participate in delinquent behavior than youths who do not enjoy family relationships. In addition, the author suggests that parents' emotional availability contributes more to youths' well-being and good behavior than does merely having parents physically present. Gilbert is a science writer for the *New York Times* and author of *A Field Guide to Boys and Girls*.

As you read, consider the following questions:
1. In the author's opinion, what parental actions result in a decrease in youths' risky behavior?
2. Why do schools' preventative measures fail, as reported by the author?
3. According to Gilbert, what activities were teens questioned about during the 1995 National Longitudinal Study of Adolescent Health?

There is no shortage of efforts in homes, schools and communities to discourage teen-agers from taking drugs, smoking, drinking or having sex. The question is, What really works? One answer, from a major study of adolescents, is that families are more important than previously thought, perhaps as important as peers.

The portion of the study's data that has been analyzed so far did not look at peer pressure, but the findings call into question the idea that peer relationships almost completely eclipse family relationships in their influence over teenagers' behavior, said Dr. Robert William Blum, one of the study's researchers and the director of the Adolescent Health Program at the University of Minnesota in Minneapolis. The primacy of peer relationships has been a widely held concept among professionals since the 1960s.

A Significant Myth

"There's been a pretty significant myth that peer groups are important and parents are not," Dr. Blum said. "We've focused so tremendously on peer pressure and instituted so many things to deal with peer pressure. And what this study is saying is that family environment matters."

The National Longitudinal Study on Adolescent Health, a survey of roughly 90,000 children, some of them 12 but a vast majority teen-agers, is the largest, most comprehensive study ever conducted on adolescent behavior in this country. It will take a decade to analyze all the data, but the first results were published on September 10, 1997, in *The Journal of the American Medical Association*.

"These findings offer the parents of America a blueprint for what works in protecting their kids from harm," said Dr. J. Richard Udry, the principal investigator and a sociologist at the Carolina Population Center of the University of North Carolina in Chapel Hill.

The most significant finding is that the teen-agers who reported feeling close to their families were the least likely to engage in any of the risky behaviors studied, which included smoking marijuana or cigarettes, drinking or having sex. Nearly as important were high expectations from the parents for their teen-agers' school performance. To a lesser degree, having a parent home at important times of day, like after school, at dinner and at bedtime, was also associated with less risky behavior.

In addition, the study identified school characteristics that were protective. Whether the school was public, parochial or private mattered less than whether the students felt that their teachers cared about them and treated them fairly.

Teens and Parent Time

A majority of American teenagers ages 12 through 15 say their top concern is not having enough time with their parents. Here are some other findings:

How teens rank barriers to spending more time with parents

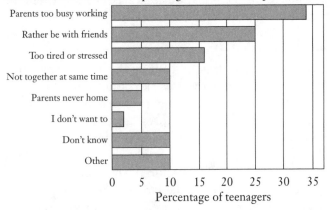

Peter King, *Christian Science Monitor*, May 3, 2000.

In an accompanying editorial, Dr. Jonathan D. Klein, a pediatrician at the University of Rochester School of Medicine and Dentistry who specializes in adolescent medicine, wrote that many of the results confirmed what other research has found, like the benefits of close ties at school and at home. "The sheer size of the study plus the opportunity to get more data are what make this study special," he said in an interview.

Where the Action Is

The survey suggests that many preventive measures used by schools and communities are misdirected, Dr. Blum said.

"Most of the rules and regulations that schools institute, like suspending students for smoking on school grounds, don't seem to have a significant impact," he said. "We invest heavily in rule development, but that's not where the action is. The action is in adults' connecting with kids."

The study began in 1995 and was conducted in three phases. In the first phase, about 90,000 students from grades 7 through 12 at 145 schools answered questionnaires about themselves.

In the second phase, interviews were conducted with about 20,000 of those students and their parents in the students' homes. To insure privacy, the students listened to questions with headphones and typed their answers into laptop computers. Students were asked about their experiences with smoking, drinking and other kinds of dangerous behavior. In the third phase, the home interviews with the teenagers were repeated a year later.

The results published in September 1997 are based on 12,118 of the initial in-home interviews. This sample was representative of the social and economic make-up of teenagers around the country.

On one level, the results are a report card on teen-agers' behavior. In the survey, 25 percent of the students said they were current smokers, 11 percent said they had smoked marijuana at least once in the past month, 17 percent reported having had alcohol more than once a month and 3 percent said they had attempted suicide in the past year. In addition, 16 percent of the 7th and 8th graders and 48 percent of those in 9th to 12th grade said they had engaged in sex.

The researchers sought to identify particular characteristics of the families, schools or students that seemed to protect against or promote risky behavior. The results were controlled for demographic characteristics like sex, race and socioeconomic status.

Certain factors correlated with lower risks in specific areas. For example, a teen-ager who had been a crime victim was more likely to be associated with violent behavior. And living in a house without easy access to alcohol, drugs, cigarettes or guns was associated with a lower likelihood of drinking, taking drugs, smoking or using guns.

Emotional Closeness and Availability

But the only factor that was linked with a lower risk across the board was a close-knit family, the study found. Emotional closeness proved more significant than the amount of time that parents spent with their teen-agers at home, calling into question a prevalent view among experts that parents can make a big difference by being home at important times of day, like after school, Dr. Blum said. Being home at such times was associated with a lower incidence of some behaviors, like smoking cigarettes or marijuana and, only among those in 9th to 12th grade, less frequent alcohol use.

"What this study showed is that it is emotional availability far more than physical presence that makes the difference," Dr. Blum said. "You need to give your kids the message that when they need to talk to you, you're available, even if it's by phone, and that they matter."

> "*Most people have no idea how pervasive
> . . . are the efforts to . . . replace parental
> influence with the influence of teachers,
> counselors and even [youths'] similarly
> immature peers.*"

Parental Influence on America's Youth Has Eroded

Thomas Sowell

Thomas Sowell is senior fellow at the Hoover Institution, a think tank based at Stanford University. Sowell contends in the following viewpoint that America's laws and educational system undermine parental influence. He believes that programs in the nation's schools, such as drug prevention and sex education, teach youths values that often conflict with those held by their parents. Because parents have been stripped of authority, they should not be held legally responsible for their children's acts, Sowell claims.

As you read, consider the following questions:

1. According to Sowell, how do books, movies, and other materials in schools portray parents?
2. In Sowell's opinion, what effect does the distribution of condoms at schools have on youths?
3. How does the author support his claim that "death education" in schools is harmful?

Of all the irrational ideas that have been thrown around in the wake of the Columbine High School shootings in Littleton, Colorado, in April 1999, one of the most reckless is the proposal to hold parents legally responsible for what their children do.

Whether the particular parents of the particular young killers [Eric Harris and Dylan Klebold] who committed this particular massacre had knowledge in advance that would make them criminally liable is something for a court of law to decide. What is at issue is whether parents in general should be held legally liable for their children's acts.

Parental Control Has Been Eroded

Responsibility and control go together. For decades now, our laws and our educational system have consistently undermined parental authority. Yet new legal responsibilities for parents are being proposed after parental control has been eroded.

Preschoolers are taught that their parents have no right to spank them. All sorts of propaganda programs in the schools—from so-called "drug prevention" to "sex education"—stress that each individual makes his or her own decisions, independently of parental or societal values.

Most people have no idea how pervasive and unremitting are the efforts to drive a wedge between children and their parents and to replace parental influence with the influence of teachers, counselors, and even the children's similarly immature peers. Many of the books, movies, and other materials used in the public schools mock parents as old windbags who are behind the times. "Trust-building" exercises teach students to rely on their classmates.

Handing out condoms in school and giving girls abortions behind their parents' backs are just isolated manifestations of this underlying philosophy, which reaches far beyond sexual matters. Nor are these just idiosyncrasies of particular teachers or schools. There are nationwide networks—some of them government-sponsored—which have disseminated pre-packaged programs designed to wean school children away from the values with which they have been raised and mold them to the values of self-anointed agents of "change."

The materials used and the things said in these materials would simply have to be seen to be believed. I certainly would never have imagined such things before doing research for my book *Inside American Education.* My assistant said she had trouble sleeping after seeing some of the movies shown to school children.

The Final Authority

Question: I disagree emphatically with what the local junior high school is teaching my daughter in sex-education class. Do I have a right to object, and how should I go about doing it?

Pediatrics professor James Dobson responds: You certainly do. I strongly support the historic American idea that parents are ultimately responsible for raising and educating their children. The school is an important ally in that effort, but the final authority lies in the home. Thus, when educational materials and content are contrary to a family's basic beliefs, parents have the right to ask school personnel to help them protect their children. Most educators are willing to accommodate the needs of individual families in this way. If they refuse, you as parents have two choices—stay and fight for what you believe, or find a new school. If you decide to oppose what is being taught, you will need the support of as many other parents as possible. Eventually you may have to take your case to the local school board. If so, be encouraged. You *can* win there. Parents in New York City became incensed over pro-homosexual materials being used in elementary schools. The superintendent and some board members refused to budge, which proved to be their undoing. Before it was over, the superintendent was fired, some board members lost their seats, and parents reestablished local control over the education of their children. Some things are worth fighting to defend. Our kids are at the top of the list.

James Dobson, *Complete Marriage and Family Home Reference Guide,* 2000.

Invasions of family privacy with diary assignments and other intrusions are all part of the same mindset. So are groups like the so-called Children's Defense Fund, which seek legal powers to impose their notions of how children should be raised. Former First Lady Hillary Clinton's pious hokum that "it takes a village" to raise a child is more of the same.

What all these efforts have in common, aside from an arrogant presumption of superiority, is a drive for power without responsibility. They don't even take responsibility for their own activities, which are hidden, denied, or camouflaged. Above all, they are not prepared to be held accountable for the consequences of their playing with children's minds.

Morality Is Optional

Columbine High School was in the news long before the recent tragic shootings there. It was featured in a *20/20* broadcast about "death education" back in 1991. This macabre subject is one of the endless procession of brainwashing programs that are taking up time sorely needed for academic work in schools across the country. One of the Columbine students who is now grown blames the course's morbid preoccupation with death for her own unsuccessful attempt at suicide.

Zealots who are pushing New Age notions of death under the guise of "education" are undeterred by parental protests that their children are having nightmares or depression. The "educators" who have been on a brainwashing ego trip have done their best to cover their own tracks.

Manuals accompanying some of these programs show how to evade and mislead parents and the public.

Running through all these programs is the notion that morality is optional: If it feels good to you, do it!

We will never know how good it felt to those young killers to shoot down those around them. Nor can we know how much the school's own reckless experiments with brainwashing contributed to the tragedy.

But it is truly galling to have those who have been undermining both morality and parents for years now demand that parents be held legally responsible for the acts of their children.

Periodical Bibliography

The following articles have been selected to supplement the diverse views presented in this chapter.

Lorraine Ali "Same Old Song: Controversy over Pop Music Is as Old as Song, but Now We're in a Cultural Arms Race," *Newsweek*, October 9, 2000.

Michael Corwin "Listen Closely and You Will Hear," *Parks & Recreation*, July 2001.

Becky Ebenkamp "Tipping the Balance," *Newsweek*, May 10, 1999.

Jan Ferrington "Are Ads Making You Sick?" *Current Health 2*, April 1999.

Thomas L. Jipping "Diagnosing the Cultural Virus," *World & I*, July 1999.

Linda Marsa "When It Comes to Drinking and Smoking, Peer Pressure Is Overrated," *Los Angeles Times*, June 25, 2001.

National Journal "Disengaged Parents, Bad Influences," July 10, 1999.

Tom Reichert "Sexy Ads Target Young Adults," *USA Today (Magazine)*, May 2001.

Janet Reitman "WARNING: Viewer Discretion Advised," *Scholastic Update*, February 22, 1999.

David E. Rosenbaum "Raw Rap and Film May Stir a Fuss, but Hist'ry Shows 'Twas Ever Thus," *New York Times*, September 21, 2000.

Sharon Waxman "Click. Bang. It's Only a Game; Video Designers Shrug Off Blame for Teen Violence," *Washington Post*, May 27, 1999.

Sue Woodman "Are You Prepared for Puberty? How to Talk to Your Child About the Pressures Ahead," *Family Life*, June 1, 2001.

What Problems Confront America's Youth?

Chapter Preface

Tragic stories about youths dying as a result of drug and alcohol abuse, gun violence, and gang activity are prevalent. However, a less known fact is that automobile accidents kill more youths than any other cause. Reporter Tod Olson claims that such fatalities are "the latest teen crisis." According to Olson, from 1991 to 2001, "60,000 kids have died on the road. That's about 3,000 more Americans than were killed in the Vietnam War in the same length of time." The American Automobile Association reports that while youths account for only 7 percent of licensed drivers, they are involved in 20 percent of reported traffic accidents.

Although some youth-related automobile fatalities involve the use of drugs and alcohol, commentators lay the blame on youths' impulsive and inexperienced driving, citing countless examples of deadly joyrides and street racing crashes. Hoping to curb the rate of such deaths, the majority of states currently enforce laws that make it more difficult for youths to earn full driving privileges. For instance, in California, young people born after 1985 must turn eighteen before they are eligible to acquire their drivers' licenses. In addition, youths acquiring their licenses must practice driving a prerequisite number of hours with an adult in the car with them. Other laws restrict the driving privileges of licensed teenagers. Some states enforce driving curfews that regulate the hours a teen can drive without adult supervision.

Proponents of stricter licensing laws insist that they save lives. The National Highway Traffic Safety Association claims that states enforcing these laws have experienced notable decreases in youth-related automobile fatalities. For instance, when the state of Georgia began suspending the licenses of young drivers for offenses such as speeding and ditching school, traffic deaths among sixteen-year-old drivers were reduced by half. James E. Hall of the National Transportation Safety Board states that these laws are needed because "current programs don't teach young people how to drive. . . . They teach them how to pass a [driving] test."

Despite strong support for stringent licensing laws, opponents argue that the laws are not effective. Some critics assert that many youth-related accidents would still take place in spite of the new restrictions, particularly curfews. For example, in Poway, California, two youths died in a noontime car crash shortly after leaving their high school campus. Obviously, nighttime curfew restrictions would not have prevented such an accident. Other commentators argue that more stringent driving laws needlessly hinder the productive pursuits of many youths. Todd Franklin of the National Motorists Association says that these laws "complicate the lives of millions of families" because many youths are employed and participate in extracurricular activities. If youths are not allowed to drive to work or other locations where they have obligations, other family members will be called upon to drive them.

Stricter licensing laws were designed to alleviate serious problems that sometimes result when young people get behind the wheel of a car. In the following chapter, authors debate other problems that affect America's youth and discuss possible solutions.

*"Illegal drug use pose[s] the greatest risk
facing the generation of youth coming of
age in the next millennium."*

Youth Substance Abuse Is a Serious Problem

Barry R. McCaffrey

In the following viewpoint, Barry R. McCaffrey maintains that as the youth population increases, proportionately more youths will abuse drugs. McCaffrey asserts that youths who actively use alcohol, tobacco, and illegal drugs are likely to experience long-term struggles with substance abuse. Therefore, he warns that failing to prevent youth substance abuse today will result in a much larger problem in the future. McCaffrey is former director of the Office of National Drug Control Policy (ONDCP). As a component of the Executive Office of the President, the ONDCP aims to reduce the trafficking, manufacturing, and use of illegal drugs.

As you read, consider the following questions:
1. In McCaffrey's view, why do two-wage-earner households present a problem for America's youths?
2. In the author's opinion, why has the use of heroin increased among youths?
3. According to the author, what drugs are popular in the "club" and "rave" scenes?

Excerpted from Barry R. McCaffrey's testimony before the Senate Committee on the Judiciary, June 17, 1998.

America's most vital resources are our young people. They are literally our future. We have no higher moral obligation than to safeguard the lives and dreams of our nation's children. The dangers of illegal drug use pose the greatest risk facing the generation of youth coming of age in the next millennium. One-in-four twelfth graders is a current user of illegal drugs. Among eighth graders the percentage of current users stands at one-in-eight. The 1996 National Household Survey (NHSDA) found that 9 percent of twelve to seventeen year olds are current drug users. While this number is well below the 1979 peak of 16.3 percent, it is still alarmingly higher than the 1992 low of 5.3 percent. A survey conducted by the Columbia University Center on Addiction and Substance Abuse found that 41 percent of teens reported attending a party where marijuana was available, and 30 percent had seen drugs sold at schools.

Youth Drug Use Trends

Moreover, because the number of young people in this nation will dramatically increase with the next generation (the "Millennium Generation"), even if we reduce the percentage of young people actively using drugs, we remain likely to be faced with increasing raw numbers of young people with initial exposure to drugs. Between 1997 and 2007, public high school enrollment will increase by roughly 13 percent. Beyond 2007, long-range projections are that births will increase by 4.2 million in 2010 and 4.6 million in 2020. Unless we can prevent this next generation from ever turning to drugs, we will face a far larger problem than we see today.

Growing numbers of two-wage-earner households and single parent families are increasing the ranks of latch-key kids. Studies show that the time periods when children are out of school and without adult supervision are the hours when they are most likely to get into trouble with drugs and other high risk behaviors. Adult—and in particular parental—involvement is critical to reducing youth drug use. With more parents working, the role of the extended family, coaches, law enforcement officers, clergy, health professionals, and other youth mentors becomes even more critical.

Marijuana Among young people, marijuana continues to be the most frequently used illegal drug. The 1997 Monitoring the Future Study (MTF) found that 49.6 percent of high school seniors reported having tried marijuana at least once—up from 41.7 percent in 1995. After six years of steady increases, the rate of current marijuana use among eighth graders fell from 11.3 percent in 1996 to 10.2 percent in 1997. However, this small shift must be put into perspective. Modest declines notwithstanding, roughly one-in-ten eighth graders have tried marijuana. We should not miss the point. Roughly 40 percent of youngsters, ages 15 to 19, who enter drug treatment have marijuana as the primary drug of abuse. This is a dangerous drug, particularly for adolescents.

Heroin Increasing rates of heroin use among youth are truly frightening. While heroin use among young people remains quite low, use among teens rose significantly in eighth, tenth, and twelfth grades during the 1990s. (However, past-year heroin use decreased among eighth graders and remained stable among tenth and twelfth graders between 1996 and 1997.) In every grade (eighth, tenth and twelfth), 2.1 percent of students have tried heroin. A frightening statistic for such a horrible drug. The heroin now being sold on America's streets has increased in purity, which allows for the drug to be snorted or smoked, as well as injected. The availability of alternative means of delivery, which young people see as less risky and more appealing than injecting, has played a major role in the increases in youth heroin use. The number of young heroin users who snort or smoke the drug continues to rise across the nation. The NHSDA found that the average age of initiation for heroin had fallen from 27.3 years old in 1988 to 19.3 in 1995.

Cocaine Cocaine use, though not prevalent among young people, is far too frequent an experience for our youth. The 1997 MTF survey found that the proportion of students reporting use of powder cocaine in the past year to be 2.2 percent, 4.1 percent, and 5 percent in grades eight, ten, and twelve, respectively. This rate represents a leveling-off in eighth-grade use and no change in tenth and twelfth grades. Among eighth graders, perceived risk also stabilized in 1997, and disapproval of use increased—both after an earlier erosion in these attitudes. The 1996 NHSDA found current use among twelve to seventeen-year-olds to be 0.6 percent, twice the rate of 1992 yet substantially lower than the 1.9 percent reported in 1985. The fact that young people are still experimenting with cocaine underscores the need for effective prevention. This requirement is substantiated by NHSDA's finding of a steady decline in the mean age of first use from 22.6 years in 1990 to 19.1 years in 1995. Crack cocaine use, according to MTF, leveled off in the eighth, tenth, and twelfth grades during the first half of the 1990s.

Other Youth Drug Trends

The 1997 MTF reports that inhalant use is most common in the eighth grade where 5.6 percent used it on a past-month basis and 11.8 percent did so on a past-year basis. Inhalants can be deadly, even with first-time use, and often represent the initial experience with illicit substances. Current use of stimulants (a category that includes methamphetamine) declined among eighth graders (from 4.6 to 3.8 percent) and tenth graders (from 5.5 percent to 5.1 percent) and increased among twelfth graders (from 4.1 to 4.8 percent). Ethnographers continue to report 'cafeteria use'—the proclivity to consume any readily available hallucinogenic, stimulant or sedative drugs like ketamine, LSD, MDMA (Ecstasy), and GHB (gamma hydroxy butrate). Young people take mood-altering pills in night clubs knowing neither what the drug is nor the dangers posed by its use alone or in combination with alcohol or other drugs. Treatment providers have noted increasing poly-drug use among young people throughout the country. NHSDA reports that the mean age of first use of hallucinogens was 17.7 years in 1995, the lowest figure since 1976.

These numbers in large part reflect the continuing popularity of drugs, such as methamphetamines, inhalants, and psychotherapeutics (tranquilizers, sedatives, analgesics, or stimulants), within the youth "club scene." Raves—late night dances, in which drug use is a prominent feature—remain popular among young people. The "rave scene," which is now firmly rooted in popular culture—from MTV to music, to movies—has been a major contributing factor to youth drug deaths in Orlando, Florida, and escalating drug use in other regions. . . .

Alcohol and Tobacco Youth drug use rates for illegal drugs, such as marijuana and heroin, are also linked to the high percentage of our young people who use tobacco. Overall, 4.5 million young people under the age of eighteen now smoke; every day another three thousand adolescents become regular smokers. One-third of these new smokers will die from tobacco-related disease. According to the NHSDA, an estimated 18 percent of young people ages twelve to seventeen are current smokers. Daily cigarette smoking rose 43 percent among high school seniors between 1992 and 1997. The 1997 MTF similarly found that daily cigarette smoking among high school seniors reached its highest level (24.6 percent) since 1979. Among eighth graders, this study found that 9 percent report smoking on a daily basis; 3.5 percent smoke a half-pack or more per day. Study after study finds a high correlation between young people who start smoking during their adolescents and then turn to other more dangerous drugs.

Foley. © 1998 by *North County Times*. Reprinted with permission.

Similar concerns are raised by the rate of underage drinking. In 1997, the MTF found that 15 percent of eighth, 25 percent of tenth, and 31 percent of twelfth graders reported binge drinking in the two weeks prior to being interviewed. The 1996 NHSDA found past-month alcohol use among 18.8 percent of twelve to seventeen year olds. New research indicates that the younger the age of drinking onset, the greater the chance that an individual at some point in life will develop a clinically defined alcohol disorder. Young people who began drinking before age fifteen were four times more likely to develop alcohol dependence than those who began drinking at age twenty-one. Among eighteen to twenty-five year olds, the number jumps to almost six-in-ten. Between 1996 and 1997, the incidence of "binge" drinking rose by 15 percent among twelve to seventeen year olds. "Heavy" drinking has increased by almost 7 percent during the same period. Here again, underage alcohol use is a risk factor that correlates with higher incidences of drug use among young people.

Attitudes Drive Actions

Youth drug use rates today are the product of attitudinal trends that experts say began in the late 1980s. (By 1990 at the latest, young people's perceptions of risk in drug use peaked and began to fall.) Most disturbing even though the average young person is not using drugs, almost one-in-four twelfth graders say that "most or all" of their friends use illegal drugs. They tend to believe that abstinence from drug use places them in the minority—something all children fear. The danger is that this false impression becomes a self-fulfilling prophecy. This misperception puts tremendous pressure on the average youth to yield to peer and societal pressures to experiment with drugs—oftentimes a tragic decision. . . .

One of the principal reasons for the alarming rate of drug use among teens is the lack of understanding within large segments of our society about the risks inherent in using illegal drugs. Movies like "Half-Baked" and others portray marijuana use as comical. Pop culture continues to both normalize and glamorize drug use. The legalizing and harm reduction crowd argues vociferously—and yet without a scintilla of factual basis—that drugs like marijuana are benign. All of this gives our young people a false sense of security about using drugs. However, the facts are that drugs are neither funny nor safe. They are tragic and deadly. . . .

Yet, the real dangers to our young people inherent in marijuana and other drug use have not yet broken through the current haze of misinformation. There is a carefully-camouflaged, exorbitantly-funded, well-heeled, elitist group whose ultimate goal is to legalize drug use in the United States. However, because the impacts of legalization—heroin being sold at the cornerstore to children with false identifications, the driver of an eighteen-wheeler high on methamphetamines traveling alongside the family minivan, skyrocketing numbers of addicts draining society of its productivity—are so horrifying to the average American, the legalizers are compelled to conceal their real objectives behind various subterfuges. (Currently, 87 percent of Americans reject legalization on its face.) Through a slick misinformation propaganda campaign these individuals perpetuate a fraud on the American people —a fraud so devious that even some of the nation's most respected newspapers and sophisticated media are capable of echoing their falsehoods.

Drugs Are Wrong

As a result, at a time when we need to be sending our young people a clear message that drugs are wrong, the message they hear is far too often muddled. We have been down this path before with disastrous results. In the 1970s and late 1980s, when we did not adequately explain to our young people the dangers of drug use, we failed our children—we allowed far too many lives to be wasted by these deadly poisons. It is incumbent upon all Americans to see these efforts for what they truly are—political movements aimed solely at legalizing drugs—and reject them outright. We need to be united as a society in making it clear to America's youth that: "Drugs destroy lives, don't let your life be wasted."

"*America's disastrous 'War on Drugs' and groups bent on reforming it are missing [the point]: the kids aren't the problem.*"

The Problem of Youth Substance Abuse Is Exaggerated

Mike Males

Mike Males is a philosophy lecturer at the University of California at Santa Cruz and author of *Framing Youth: 10 Myths About the Next Generation*. In the following viewpoint, Males argues that substance abuse is a far greater problem for adults than it is for youths. For example, only seven of Chicago's nine hundred drug overdose deaths in 1999 were adolescents. Males concludes that the focus on youth substance abuse has diverted attention from the larger problem of substance abuse among adults, resulting in the failure of America's drug war.

As you read, consider the following questions:

1. According to Males, how did the youths he interviewed in a Chicago correction center respond to the question of why so few youths die from drugs?
2. In Males's view, what did the 2000 Monitoring the Future Survey reveal about youths' attitudes regarding tobacco and alcohol?
3. How does American teens' use of tobacco, alcohol, and illicit substances compare to that of Dutch youths, according to the author?

From "The Drug Debate Gets Dopier," by Mike Males, www.alternet.org, August 20, 2001. Copyright © 2001 by Independent Media Institute. Reprinted with permission.

When I asked an assembly of 300 youths locked in Chicago's mammoth juvenile prison why so few kids die from drugs (only seven of the city's 900 overdose deaths in 1999 were teens), several shouted: "Because you don't die from weed!" That's the point both America's disastrous "War on Drugs" and groups bent on reforming it are missing: the kids aren't the problem. Yet, respected drug policy reform advocates like the Lindesmith Center now insist that stopping teenage drug use should be our most urgent policy priority. Lindesmith and other reformers claim that if drugs were legalized for adults and regulated like cigarettes and beer, teens who now freely acquire marijuana and ecstasy through illicit dealers would find the stuff harder to get.

"Protect the Children" Stratagem

Lindesmith researcher Robert Sharpe recently wrote Ann Landers that The Netherlands' policy of legalizing marijuana with "age controls" has "reduced overall drug use" and "protect(ed) children from drugs." Common Sense for Drug Policy sensibly argues for prioritizing addiction treatment but still urges a tripling in spending to promote teenage abstinence. The National Organization for the Reform of Marijuana Laws (NORML), Marijuana Policy Project (MPP), and Change the Climate argue that "responsible adults" should be allowed to use marijuana while "minors" should be prohibited. (If honest, they'd emphasize that parents who use drugs, alcohol, or tobacco greatly multiply the odds their kids will, too.) Drug reform groups praised "Traffic" (the Drug-Enforcement-Administration-endorsed movie that featured black and brown pushers supplying upscale white kids) largely because of its absurd line that teens score heroin easier than legal, "regulated" alcohol.

Reformers, before their latest "protect the children" stratagem, used to argue that legal, government-regulated alcohol and tobacco were teenagers' big drugs-of-choice. True enough. The 2000 Monitoring the Future survey shows teens at every age believe alcohol and tobacco are far easier to get than every type of illicit drug. Their speculation is confirmed by surveys showing American teens use legal, age-regulated alcohol and tobacco 2.5 to 100 times more than illicit marijuana, ecstasy, or heroin.

The realities of The Netherlands' drug policy reforms are distorted both by American Drug War officials (such as former czar Barry McCaffrey, who mendaciously depicted Holland, whose homicide rate is one-eighth the U.S.'s, as awash in murder and crime) and by drug-reform groups. Unfortunately, American reformers who exploit fear of teenage drug experimentation in order to win legal highs for more addiction-plagued grownups are pursuing a strategy opposite to that Dutch reformers used: calming fear of youthful soft-drug use in order to redirect attention to treating middle-aged hard-drug addicts. Contrary to Lindesmith's argument that protecting "children" from their own drug use should be the "primary mandate" of drug policy, the Dutch implemented successful reforms precisely because they DIDN'T panic over teens and pot.

It's a Wash

In fact, The Netherlands' Trimbos Research Institute found marijuana use by Dutch 12–18 year-olds tripled from 3 percent in 1988 to 11 percent in 1996, then fell to 9 percent in 1999. Teenage marijuana use also grew in the 1990s in the United States and other prohibitionist countries, where anti-drug education and penalties escalated. The U.S. National Household Survey on Drug Abuse found 12–17 year-olds' monthly pot smoking rose from 5 percent in 1988 to 8 percent in 1996, where it remained in 1999.

Youth Alcohol Use Decreasing					
% Annual Use—Alcohol					
	96–97	97–98	98–99	99–00	00–01
Grades 6–12	58.3	56.9	56.8	53.3	52.1

14th Annual Pride Survey, *Alcoholism & Drug Abuse Weekly*, July 23, 2001.

Allowing for slight differences in trend timing and age groups surveyed, it's a wash. Dutch teens use marijuana, heroin, cocaine, and ecstasy at about the same rates as U.S. teens. Dutch teens use legal alcohol and cigarettes much more, as they always have. But use statistics don't matter.

The important issue is that neither Dutch nor American teens show appreciable or increasing drug abuse. In both countries, teens under age 20 comprise only about 3 percent of drug abuse deaths, with the vast bulk of drug abuse occurring among adults 30 and older.

Thus, neither benign Dutch legalization nor draconian U.S. prohibition (billion-dollar anti-drug campaigns, tens of millions of arrests, skyrocketing imprisonment, military interventions) had any material effect on teenage drug decisions. In New York, Mayor Rudolph Giuliani's police vans hauled away tens of thousands of roachclippers; in San Francisco, marijuana possession arrests declined sharply from the 1980s to the 1990s and private pot smoking is effectively decriminalized. The effect on teens? Nada. In The Netherlands and U.S., New York and San Francisco, teenage drug use and abuse patterns are identical. Obsession with every up-down tick in drug use surveys reflects the inflated self-importance drug-war combatants attach to their irrelevant squabble over whose policy would make youths just say no.

The larger point is that the Dutch decriminalization and harm-reduction reforms did contribute to dramatic reductions in drug abuse among mostly-older addicts. Dutch heroin deaths dropped by 40 percent from the late 1970s to the late 1990s while they tripled in the U.S. In America, 1999 and 2000 Drug Abuse Warning Network reports show hospital emergency treatments and deaths from drug overdoses soared to their highest levels ever. From 1999 to 2000, U.S. hospital emergencies involving cocaine increased 4 percent, heroin rose 15 percent, and methamphetamine leaped 29 percent, all reaching record peaks. Today, Americans are dying from heroin, cocaine, and speed at rates seven times higher than the Dutch. The point drug reformers should be stressing is that The Netherlands' "protects children" NOT by chasing around teens who smoke pot, but by reducing the devastating damage hard-drug addicts inflict on themselves and their families, communities, and kids.

Misplaced Conjectures About Youths

Both the appalling failure of America's War on Drugs to stem drug abuse and the encouraging realities of the Dutch reforms validate the latter's harm-reduction approach more convincingly than misplaced conjectures about youths. Teenagers are not waiting with baited bong for the latest official "message" or "policy." Real-life lessons are far more compelling. Teenagers' avoidance of hard drugs and moderate patronage of soft drugs appears a generally healthy reaction to the alarming damage they see hard-drug abuse causing adults around them.

Lindesmith's excellent "Marijuana Myths, Marijuana Facts" scrutinizes hundreds of studies and government-commissioned reports that consistently "have documented the drug's relative harmlessness." Nowhere does Lindesmith's exhaustive research summary reveal any medical, developmental, or other reason why adults should be allowed to use marijuana responsibly but teenagers should be prohibited. Nor do Lindesmith, NORML, MPP, and other drug-reform groups explain why they're adamant that adolescent use of a "relatively harmless" drug should remain illegal or why they'd continue subjecting teens to the dangers they attribute to prohibition. For example, reformers' adults-only marijuana and ecstasy legalization scheme might assure safer supplies for grownups, but youths still would have to patronize illicit markets where hard drugs and contaminated knockoffs abound. The moralistic stance that widespread, moderate marijuana and ecstasy use by teens should remain outlawed absent solid evidence of harm sabotages "harm reduction" strategies, since harm-reducers risk punishment if they help youths break laws.

Young age is a politically convenient target for emotional crusading, but it is not a valid criterion for discrimination. Until the calming facts debunking irrational fears surrounding modern adolescents and drugs become more known and accepted, marijuana decriminalization will not happen. Lindesmith's and other reformers' campaign to "protect children" from their own drug use slants science to the point that many "fact sheets" drug reformers present selectively choose and omit "facts" just as Drug War propaganda does. And, like the Drug War's overriding precept, reformers' youth-prohibition stance upholds the myth that drugs are a menace of marginalized subgroups when, in truth, America's real illicit-drug crisis is mainstream, middle-American, and middle-aged.

| "*Teen pregnancy has serious consequences for the teen mother, the child, and to society in general.*"

Teenage Pregnancy Is a Serious Problem

National Campaign to Prevent Teen Pregnancy

The National Campaign to Prevent Teen Pregnancy (NCPTP) is an organization that aims to promote the health and well-being of children, youths, and families by reducing the rate of teenage pregnancy. In Part I of the following viewpoint, the campaign claims that pregnancy has more negative consequences for teenage girls than for older women. For instance, the organization asserts that, compared to older women, pregnancy carries more health risks for teenagers. Furthermore, children of teenage mothers also suffer more health risks than the children of older mothers. In Part II, the NCPTP examines the ways in which the incidence of teenage pregnancy can be reduced, such as making contraceptives available to youths.

As you read, consider the following questions:
1. According to the organization, what are some of the health risks for pregnant teens?
2. In the NCPTP's opinion, why do children of teenage parents receive inadequate parenting?
3. How does the organization support its claim that the media influence teenage pregnancy?

Part I: Excerpted from "Teen Pregnancy—So What?" by the National Campaign to Prevent Teen Pregnancy, www.teenpregnancy.org, 2001. Copyright © 2001 by the National Campaign to Prevent Teen Pregnancy. Reprinted with permission. Part II: Excerpted from "Get Organized: A Guide to Ending Teen Pregnancy," by the National Campaign to Prevent Teen Pregnancy, www.teenpregnancy.com, 1999. Copyright © 1999 by the National Campaign to Prevent Teen Pregnancy. Reprinted with permission.

I

Reducing the nation's rate of teen pregnancy is one of the most strategic and direct means available to improve overall child well-being and to reduce persistent child poverty. Teen pregnancy has serious consequences for the teen mother, the child, and to society in general.

Despite the recently declining teen pregnancy rates, 4 in 10 teenage girls get pregnant at least once before they reach age 20, resulting in more than 900,000 teen pregnancies a year. At this level, the United States has the highest rate of teen pregnancy in the fully industrialized world.

Bad for the Mother

• *Future prospects for teenagers decline significantly if they have a baby.* Teen mothers are less likely to complete school and more likely to be single parents. Less than one-third of teens who begin their families before age 18 ever earn a high school diploma.

• *There are serious health risks for adolescents who have babies.* Young adolescents (particularly those under age 15) experience a maternal death rate 2.5 times greater than that of mothers aged 20–24. Common medical problems among adolescent mothers include poor weight gain, pregnancy-induced hypertension, anemia, sexually transmitted diseases (STDs), and cephalopelvic disproportion. Later in life, adolescent mothers tend to be at greater risk for obesity and hypertension than women who were not teenagers when they had their first child.

• *Teen pregnancy is closely linked to poverty and single parenthood.* A 1990 study showed that almost one-half of all teenage mothers and over three-quarters of unmarried teen mothers began receiving welfare within five years of the birth of their first child. The growth in single-parent families remains the single most important reason for increased poverty among children over the last twenty years, as documented in the 1998 Economic Report of the President. Out-of-wedlock childbearing (as opposed to divorce) is currently the driving force behind the growth in the number of single parents, and half of first out-of-wedlock births are to teens. Therefore, reducing teen pregnancy and child-bearing is an obvious place to anchor serious efforts to reduce poverty in future generations.

Bad for the Child

• *Children born to teen mothers suffer from higher rates of low birth weight and related health problems.* The proportion of babies with low birth weights born to teens is 28 percent higher than the proportion for mothers age 20–24. Low birth weight raises the probabilities of infant death, blindness, deafness, chronic respiratory problems, mental retardation, mental illness, and cerebral palsy. In addition, low birth weight doubles the chances that a child will later be diagnosed as having dyslexia, hyperactivity, or another disability.

• *Children of teens often have insufficient health care.* Despite having more health problems than the children of older mothers, the children of teen mothers receive less medical care and treatment. In his or her first 14 years, the average child of a teen mother visits a physician and other medical providers an average of 3.8 times per year, compared with 4.3 times for a child of older childbearers. And when they do visit medical providers, more of the expenses they incur are paid by others in society. One recent study suggested that the medical expenses paid by society would be reduced dramatically if teenage mothers were to wait until they were older to have their first child.

• *Children of teen mothers often receive inadequate parenting.* Children born to teen mothers are at higher risk of poor parenting because their mothers—and often their fathers as well—are typically too young to master the demanding job of being a parent. Still growing and developing themselves, teen mothers are often unable to provide the kind of environment that infants and very young children require for optimal development. Recent research, for example, has clarified the critical importance of sensitive parenting and early cognitive stimulation for adequate brain development. Given the importance of careful nurturing and stimulation in the first three years of life, the burden born by babies with parents who are too young to be in this role is especially great.

• *Children with adolescent parents often fall victim to abuse and neglect.* A recent analysis found that there are 110 re-

Pregnant Again

Percent of births to teenagers who were already mothers (by state or district)

1.	Wash., D.C.	28.0 pct.
2.	Mississippi	24.4 pct.
3.	Texas	24.1 pct.
4.	Georgia	24.1 pct.
5.	Arkansas	23.5 pct.
6.	Illinois	23.4 pct.
7.	Alabama	23.0 pct.
8.	Nevada	22.8 pct.
9.	Louisiana	22.7 pct.
10.	Florida	22.5 pct.

U.S. News & World Report, March 5, 2001.

ported incidents of abuse and neglect per 1,000 families headed by a young teen mother. By contrast, in families where the mothers delay childbearing until their early twenties, the rate is less than half this level—or 51 incidents per 1,000 families. Similarly, rates of foster care placement are significantly higher for children whose mothers are under 18. In fact, over half of foster care placements of children with these young mothers could be averted by delaying child-bearing, thereby saving taxpayers nearly $1 billion annually in foster care costs alone.

• *Children of teenagers often suffer from poor school performance.* Children of teens are 50 percent more likely to repeat a grade; they perform much worse on standardized tests; and ultimately they are less likely to complete high school than if their mothers had delayed childbearing.

Bad for Us All

• *The U.S. still leads the fully industrialized world in teen pregnancy and birth rates—by a wide margin.* In fact, the U.S. rates are nearly double Great Britain's, at least four times those of France and Germany, and more than ten times that of Japan.

• *Teen pregnancy costs society billions of dollars a year.* There are nearly half a million children born to teen mothers each year. Most of these mothers are unmarried, and many will end up poor and on welfare. Each year the federal government alone spends about $40 billion to help families that began with a teenage birth.

• *Teen pregnancy hurts the business community's "bottom line."* Too many children start school unprepared to learn, and teachers are overwhelmed trying to deal with problems that start in the home. Forty-five percent of first births in the United States are to women who are either unmarried, teenagers, or lacking a high school degree, which means that too many children—tomorrow's workers—are born into families that are not prepared to help them succeed. In addition, teen mothers often do not finish high school themselves. It's not easy for a teen to learn work skills and be a dependable employee while caring for children.

• *A new crop of kids becomes teenagers each year.* This means that prevention efforts must be constantly renewed and reinvented. And between 1995 and 2010, the number of girls aged 15–19 is projected to increase by 2.2 million.

II

Research has identified a host of factors—related to individual behavior, family and community situations, and cultural pressures—that contribute to teen pregnancy. Most programs to prevent teen pregnancy focus on one of these groups of factors.

Behavior and Risk-Taking

Teens who get pregnant or cause a pregnancy are often engaged in a pattern of poor choices. Teens who use or abuse drugs and alcohol, who have had a history of violence and delinquency, or are failing at or dropped out of school have higher rates of sexual activity. Teens using drugs and alcohol are more likely to put themselves in sexually risky situations and are much less likely to use contraception. Teen girls whose first partners are older teens or adult men are also less likely to use contraception and are more likely to report that their first sexual experience was involuntary or unwanted. And, teens who begin intercourse at a young age have a higher risk of getting pregnant or causing a pregnancy.

Giving teens the skills and motivation to make informed decisions about sexuality can reduce sexual risk-taking.

Helping teens avoid other risk-taking behaviors may also help teens avoid a pregnancy.

The Environment

The environments that children grow up in have an important influence on their risk of teen pregnancy. As [researcher D. Kirby] recently wrote:

"Research shows that youths at greatest risk [for teen pregnancy] are more likely to live in areas with: high poverty rates, low levels of education, high residential turnover, and high divorce rates. Their parents are more likely to have low levels of education, to be poor, to have experienced a divorce or separation, or to never have married, and their mothers and older sisters are more likely to have given birth as adolescents."

Increasing the capacity of families and communities to nurture teens and help them stay in school and set goals for their lives may contribute to lower rates of teen pregnancy. Young people who feel supported by parents, school, and community during their adolescence are buffered against the risk of too-early pregnancy.

Cultural and Media Messages

Teens are barraged by TV shows, films, songs, and advertising in which sex has little meaning, unplanned pregnancy seldom happens, and sexual partners are rarely married, let alone committed to each other. Sexual themes permeate the pictures and plot lines. Teens may spend more time in the presence of these messages than in the presence of alternative messages that value staying in school and preparing for adulthood.

Teen pregnancy is just one problem young people face in our culture today—and perhaps not the most pressing one. Parents identify violence, gangs, drugs, and pressure from peers to engage in unhealthy behaviors as even greater risks than early pregnancy.

Communities can help prevent teen pregnancy even when that issue is not the primary focus of an initiative. Pregnancy prevention can be adopted as part of a strategy that focuses on more immediate concerns of that community.

Categories of Prevention

Most teen pregnancy prevention programs have emphasized education, skills, abstinence, and access to contraception. However, the definition of what constitutes teen pregnancy prevention is best expanded to include activities that seek to instill teens with confidence and a sense of the future. This speaks to motivation to avoid pregnancy, a critical element in a pregnancy-free adolescence.

Many different kinds of programs exist to help teens avoid pregnancy. They can be divided into several categories:

- education for teens about sex, relationships, pregnancy, and parenthood;
- reproductive health services for teens;
- programs to strengthen teens' bonds with family and community;
- youth development and school-to-career programs;
- media campaigns; and
- multiple component campaigns.

*"Teen childbearing . . . does impose some
additional penalties. But the great divide
regarding . . . well-being is clearly between
single and married mothers."*

Unwed Motherhood Is a More Serious Problem than Teenage Pregnancy

Maggie Gallagher

In the following viewpoint, Maggie Gallagher contends that
pregnant teenagers' failure to marry—not teen pregnancy
itself—is a serious problem. Gallagher argues that all young
unwed mothers—not just teens—suffer from more depression and poverty than their married counterparts. She asserts that when young women decide to raise children without the financial benefits that marriage confers, they are
merely responding to American society's disapproval of early
marriage. Gallagher is an affiliate scholar at the Institute for
American Values, a private, nonpartisan organization that
promotes marriage and family-oriented values.

As you read, consider the following questions:
1. In what ways are unwed teenage mothers and unwed
   mothers in their early twenties similar, as stated by
   Gallagher?
2. According to the author, what do many educators think
   about early marriage?
3. How does the author support her view that teenage
   marriages can succeed?

Excerpted from *The Age of Unwed Mothers: Is Teen Pregnancy the Problem?* by
Maggie Gallagher (New York: Institute for American Values, 1999). Copyright
© 1999 by the Institute for American Values. Reprinted with permission.

Here is the paradox. As a society, we aim a fair amount of public money and many strong words at the problem of "teen pregnancy," that is, at the 376,000 births in one recent year to single teen mothers under the age of 20. Yet we pay comparatively little attention—indeed, it often seems that as a society we are stone-cold silent—regarding the 439,000 births that same year to single mothers in their early 20s. Are we against the former but indifferent to the latter? If so, what is our reasoning? Consider the prospects for a typical 20- or 22-year-old single mother and her baby. Are they really that much different, or better, than those facing an 18-or 19-year-old single mother?

Just waiting for a few more birthdays to roll around before having a child does not reduce the risk to mother or child by much, at least for older teen moms. Researchers comparing the fate of sisters, for example, concluded that national estimates of the effects of unwed teen childbearing may have been exaggerated. Why? One reason is that many of these young women who avoided "teen" childbearing then had children out of wedlock in their 20s. Other recent studies have found that single adult mothers resemble single teen mothers more than they resemble adult married mothers. In one 1996 study, Marguerite Stevenson Bratt explains, "adolescent mothers experience significantly more mental health problems and significantly less well-being than married adult mothers but report similar levels of psychological adjustment when compared to single adult mothers."

The Great Divide

Teen childbearing, as opposed to adult unmarried childbearing, does impose some additional penalties. But the great divide regarding economic status and emotional well-being is clearly between single and married mothers. How much will waiting a few years to become an unwed mother help a teenager economically? When it comes to family income, not much, according to a recent analysis: "The economic situation of older, single childbearers is meager at best; their situation is much closer to that of teen mothers than that of married childbearers. . . . "

A wealth of evidence accumulated in the 1990s has produced a new consensus among most family scholars that marriage matters. Overall, children raised by single parents are five times as likely to be poor, twice as likely to drop out of school, and two to three times more likely as adults to commit crimes leading to an incarceration. These children are also more likely to be victims of crime, especially child abuse. Even after controlling not only for socioeconomic variables (parental education, occupation, family income, welfare receipt, and race), but also for family process variables (parental warmth, discipline, and time spent with children), "the net effects of non-intact family structure on child development outcomes are negative and strong," according to Lingxin Hao of Johns Hopkins University. Urie Bronfenbrenner, one of the nation's leading family scholars, sums it up: "Controlling for associated factors such as low income, children growing up in such [father-absent] households are at greater risk for experiencing a variety of behavioral and educational problems, including extremes of hyperactivity or withdrawal, lack of attentiveness in the classroom, difficulty in deferring gratification, impaired academic achievement, school misbehavior, absenteeism, dropping out, involvement in socially alienated peer groups, and, especially, the so-called 'teenage syndrome' of behaviors that tend to hang together—smoking, drinking, early and frequent sexual experience, a cynical attitude toward work, adolescent pregnancy, and, in the more extreme cases, drugs, suicide, vandalism, violence, and criminal acts."

That unmarried birth rates among older teens are so similar to those of women in their early 20s should alert us to an important possibility. Perhaps the teens who are becoming single mothers are responding not only to specific conditions affecting their age group, but also, and even especially, to broader cultural messages influencing all young women. In short, perhaps our "teen pregnancy" problem stems from a larger issue that we have yet to confront. That issue is the weakening of norms connecting marriage to childbearing throughout our society. Are we transmitting a marriage culture to the next generation? Do we want to? What can we say or do to encourage more girls and young women to see a good marriage, a committed partner and father, and not just an 18th or a 20th birthday, as the thing worth waiting for? . . .

The Marriage Dimension

Young adult women having children is not a new phenomenon. The number of women who had their first child during their teen years was almost the same in the early 1970s as in the early 1990s. But the proportion of teen moms who conceived their first child out of wedlock has increased significantly, rising from about 65 percent in 1970–74 to 89 percent in 1990–94. The single biggest change in recent decades has been the declining proportion of pregnant single teens who marry. . . .

Why do the dreams and desires of young pregnant women today so often fail to include a husband? Even if fewer pregnant women today are pushed into marriage by social pressure, why are so few *pulled* into marriage by the powerful advantages, both for themselves and their children, of marriage over unwed motherhood?

It's not that young unwed mothers are hostile to or uninterested in marriage. In a study of a nationally representative sample of young people, drawn from the National Longitudinal Survey of Youth, unmarried mothers were found to be no less interested in marriage than women who had not experienced a premarital birth. Despite the prevalence of casual sex, young women still tend to have the babies of men with whom they are in love.

One study finds that, even though most school-age mothers had sex the first time for reasons other than love, more than 80 percent of both Black and White teen mothers said that they were in love with their partners at the time of conception. Most of the mothers hoped to marry the father. A recent report on fragile families—poor inner-city, unwed, minority couples with children—finds that 70 percent of these couples, questioned soon after the baby's birth, say that there is at least a fifty-fifty chance they will marry.

Another study of teen parents from the Pacific Northwest, the majority of whom were White and from homes that were not currently welfare-dependent, finds that three-fourths of these teen mothers were either "planning to marry" or "going steady" with the father at the time of the birth. Yet most of them, of course, do not get married. In another sample of mostly White, working-class, rural teen mothers, about one in five described herself as "engaged." Many were cohabiting with the fathers of their children. Why aren't they wed?

What are they waiting for? What encourages so many young women to fall in love with men, to have babies with them, and to live with them, but to stop short of getting married? The data clearly show that the dream of marriage remains powerful, even for girls and young women in disadvantaged circumstances. But with each passing year, fewer young women, especially young mothers, realize this dream. Current research, in our view, has not adequately examined or explained this phenomenon.

Ramirez. © 1992 by Copley News Service. Reprinted with permission.

Perhaps some of these mothers cannot convince the fathers to marry. One study argues that, following the legalization of abortion in the early 1970s, many pregnant women who wanted marriage became less able to persuade their partners to see things their way. On the other hand, in another study of a group of White unwed teen mothers, about

44 percent of the teens said that they and their boyfriends had jointly considered marriage, but rejected it. Only 18 percent of these teen mothers reported that they had wanted to get married, but that the fathers had refused. Nearly 30 percent said that they had never considered marriage. . . .

The Campaign Against Marriage

One infrequently acknowledged reason why fewer young mothers get married these days is that they are actively discouraged from doing so. As a society, our disapproval of early marriage has become ever sharper and more powerful, while our worries about unwed parenthood have become comparatively vague. In brief, perhaps young unwed mothers are not so much rebelling against, as conforming to, prevailing social norms.

Consider the extreme scarcity of community and church programs aimed at helping unwed couples with children create good marriages. (Have you ever come across one?) Surely this absence is largely the result of overwhelming expert and community disapproval of early marriage as an answer to the risks posed by non-marital pregnancies. In these sorts of ways, our campaign against teen marriage has been much more thorough, and far more successful, than our campaign against teen pregnancy.

As [history professor] Maris Vinovskis points out, researchers and other experts during the past 25 years have actively discouraged looking at early marriage as anything other than a serious social problem, despite the relative lack of data comparing the consequences of early marriage to the consequences of early unwed motherhood. Here is a 1973 conclusion, typical and quite speculative, from two influential researchers, L.V. Klerman and J.F. Jeckel: "[E]arly marriages have not proved stable. . . . It therefore appears unwise to encourage teenagers to marry to legalize their sexual activity or their offspring. The rapid making and dissolution of a marriage with all its legal and financial complications may be more of a psychic trauma to the mother and her child than an attempt to raise a child within her parent's home or independently, or attempt to live unmarried in a temporary but loving relationship with a man."

Similarly, as reported in the *New York Times*, a social worker in a home for pregnant girls reported in 1972 that "the feeling here is that an early marriage . . . is not advisable."

School counselors have also made preventing marriage one of their explicit goals when counseling pregnant students. A 1973 paper on school-based programs for pregnant teens proudly asserts that "counseling services . . . can reduce the number of inappropriate marriages, diminish the number of repeat pregnancies, and help direct young mothers toward more satisfying lives." More recently, a 1992 RAND (Research and Development Institute) study reports that many educators "applaud the decreasing incidence of marriage," citing studies "indicating that early and precipitous marriage usually worsens the long-term outlook for the teenage mother and her child.". . .

The Benefits of Marriage

When early marriages survive, the benefits to a young woman are substantial. Most obviously, she benefits from her husband's earnings and the gradual accumulation of wealth that is typical of married couples, but not cohabiting couples, and not single mothers.

The independent importance of marriage in increasing the incomes of young mothers is suggested by a national study of single women age 16–22 who had their first birth in the 1970s and early 1980s. Five to seven years later, when those children were entering school, fewer than a third of these mothers were generating enough income on their own (including child support payments and help from relatives) to avoid poverty. The mother's age at birth seemed to have no effect: mothers who had first given birth in their early 20s were no better (or worse) off than mothers who had first given birth as teenagers.

Financially, for this group of mothers, the great divide was between the roughly 50 percent who had married and the 50 percent who had not. When husbands' earnings were taken into account, the proportion of these mothers who were able to avoid poverty increased from less than a third to more than 60 percent. Even though only half of the women had married, husbands' earnings caused the average annual family income for the sample as a whole to more than double.

For children, as well, the advantages stemming from a mother's choice of marriage over unwed motherhood are impressive. Even brief marriages may yield benefits for children. For example, marriage seems to protect young mothers against depression. One nationally representative study finds that, among White 18 and 19 year olds, about 41 percent of unmarried, first-time mothers reported many symptoms of depression, compared to 28 percent of married, primiparous mothers of that age. Maternal depression is a significant risk factor for children, often leading to problems in adjustment that may linger for years after the mother's recovery.

Can teen marriages succeed? Several studies suggest that, even in the most disadvantaged circumstances, a surprising number of young marriages do succeed. In one study, 85 percent of all 18- and 19-year-old brides were still living with their husbands five years later. Another analysis finds that, among Whites, 75 percent of young pregnant women who married before the birth were still married ten years later. . . .

Inseparable from the Marriage Problem

The teen pregnancy problem in our society is inseparable from a much larger marriage problem. Changing *adult* ideas about marriage and its relationship to procreation have directly guided the entire cluster of trends in teen behavior—including rising rates of unmarried sex, weak motivation to use contraceptives, rising ages at marriage, and sharp declines in both legitimation and adoption—that we currently describe, somewhat misleadingly, as our crisis of teen pregnancy.

Some three decades into the divorce revolution, we Americans have much less faith in the idea that marriage changes reality: that the institution is bigger than the couple and that the institution can, independently, as it were, help guide the couple toward a successful union. Most of our parents and grandparents had that faith. Many of us are losing it. Many of our teenage children would not even recognize the idea.

For a young woman today who does not see marriage as an essential support to her motherhood, or who does not foresee much possibility of making a good marriage in the future, the decision to become a single mother at age 18 or 19 is not especially irrational or hard to understand. If it is not marriage that confers special meaning to the sexual act, then perhaps it is her giving the gift of unprotected sex, or making a baby. If it is not marriage that a young woman is waiting for before becoming a mother, then how much difference will a few more years of waiting really make?

To a degree that might make many of us uncomfortable, when young women today prefer unwed motherhood over adoption or early marriage, they have not been ignoring adult counsel. They have been heeding it.

Why should a teenager postpone having a baby? What our society as a whole, and especially our "teen pregnancy" rhetoric, currently tells these young people—until you reach age 20, having a baby is a huge mistake, as is getting married, but after that, it's up to you—is not likely to capture their moral imagination. Does it capture yours?

"Weapon-carrying, and guns in particular, among youths has been identified as a key factor in the recent increase in youth violence."

Youth Gun Violence Is a Serious Problem

Randy M. Page and Jon Hammermeister

In the following viewpoint, Randy M. Page and Jon Hammermeister suggest that the increasing availability of guns has resulted in more youth violence. Page and Hammermeister assert that youths who carry guns are often involved in criminal activities despite their claims of carrying firearms for self-defense. The authors suggest that society must take measures to control the availability of guns. Page lectures in health and safety at the University of Idaho at Moscow. Hammermeister is an instructor in the Department of Health and Human Performance at Central Community College in Bend, Oregon.

As you read, consider the following questions:
1. In the authors' view, what behaviors are guns associated with in inner-city schools?
2. What are the disadvantages of placing metal detectors in schools, as stated by Page and Hammermeister?
3. What are three ways that society can control the availability of guns, as suggested by the authors?

A higher incidence of weapon-carrying, and guns in particular, among youths has been identified as a key factor in the recent increase in youth violence. Weapon-carrying increases risk of death and serious injury to both the carrier and others. In recent years a number of studies have investigated the accessibility of weapons and the extent to which youth carry them.

According to the 1990 Youth Risk Behavior Survey, 1 in 20 senior high school students carried a firearm, usually a handgun, and 1 in 5 carried a weapon of some type during the 30 days preceding the survey. A survey of 10 inner-city high schools in four states found that 35% of male and 11% of female students reported carrying a gun. A study of rural school students in southeast Texas found that 6% of male students had taken guns to school, and almost 2% reported that they did so almost every day. In addition, 42.3% of those surveyed said they could get a gun if they wanted one. More than one-third (34%) of urban high school students in Seattle reported having easy access to handguns, while 11.4% of males and 1.5% of females reported owning a handgun. One-third of those who owned handguns reported that they had fired at someone. Further, almost 10% of female students reported a firearm homicide or suicide among family members or close friends. Another study from the southeast U.S. found that 9% of urban and suburban youth owned a handgun.

A poll of students in grades six through twelve conducted by [professor] Louis Harris for the Harvard School of Public Health in 1993 found that 59% said they could get a handgun if they wanted one, and 21% said they could get one within the hour. More than 60% of urban youth reported that they could get a handgun, and 58% of suburban youth also claimed that they could. Fifteen percent of students reported carrying a handgun in the past month, 11% said that they had been shot at, 9% said that they had fired a gun at someone, and 4% said they had carried a gun to school in the past year.

In a study of two public inner-city junior high schools in Washington, D.C., 47% of males reported having ever carried knives, and 25% reported having ever carried guns for protection or to use in case they got into a fight; 37% of females reported having carried a knife for these purposes. Both schools are located in high-crime areas.

Why Do Young People Carry Weapons?

A common reason given by young people for carrying weapons is for protection against being "jumped." However, research has shown that weapon-carrying among youth appears to be more closely associated with criminal activity, delinquency, and aggressiveness than to purely defensive behavior. Handgun ownership by inner-city high school youth has been associated with gang membership, selling drugs, interpersonal violence, being convicted of crimes, and either suspension or expulsion from school. Gun-carrying among junior high students is also strongly linked with indicators of serious delinquency, such as having been arrested. [According to researchers D.W. Webster, P.S. Painer, and H.R. Champion,] these studies have the following implications for the prevention of gun-carrying among youth:

A Continuing and Serious Threat

A continuing and serious threat of school shootings and other youth violence is deeply rooted in unhealthy attitudes about violence and easy access to guns, according to a Josephson Institute of Ethics survey of more than 15,000 teenagers. In issuing the first of a series of reports based on a national survey administered in 2000, Michael Josephson, the Institute's president, said, "The seeds of violence can be found in schools all over America. Today's teens, especially boys, have a high propensity to use violence when they are angry, they have easy access to guns, drugs and alcohol, and a disturbing number take weapons to school."

Michael Josephson, *Josephson Institute 2000 Report Card on the Ethics of American Youth: Report #1*, April 1, 2001.

If gun-carrying stems largely from antisocial attitudes and behaviors rather than from purely defensive motives of otherwise nonviolent youths, interventions designed to prevent delinquency may be more effective than those that focus only on educating youths about the risks associated with carrying a gun. The latter may, however, be able to deter less hardened youths from carrying weapons in the future. Intensive and comprehensive interventions directed at high-risk children could possibly "inoculate" children against the many social factors that foster criminal deviance and the most violent behavior patterns.

Adult criminals and youth involved in illegal activities have reported that guns are not difficult to obtain. Illegal or unregulated transactions are the primary sources of guns used in violent acts; stealing, borrowing from friends or acquaintances, and illegal purchasing of guns are the most common. Less than 1 in 5 guns used for illegal activities were purchased from licensed dealers. The most commonly cited reason for acquiring a gun is "self-defense.". . .

Firearm Violence and Youth

Among teenagers 15–19 years of age and young adults 20–24 years of age, 1 of every 4 deaths is by a firearm. One of every 8 deaths in children 10–14 is by a firearm. For those 15–19 there are substantial variations by race and sex in the percentage of deaths due to firearms. Among African-American teenage males, 60% of deaths result from firearm injury compared with 23% of white teenage males. Among African-American teenage females it is 22% compared with 10% of white female teenagers. The number of African-American males aged 15–19 who died from gunshot wounds in 1990 was nearly five times higher than the number who died from AIDS, sickle-cell disease, and all other natural causes combined.

In 1990, 82% of all homicide victims aged 15–19 (91% and 77% African-American and white males, respectively) and 76% of victims aged 20–24 (87% and 71% among African-American and white males, respectively) were killed with guns. Firearm homicide for African-American males 15–19 years of age was 11 times the rate among white males, 105.3 compared with 9.7 per 100,000 population. The rate for African-American females was five times the rate for white females, 10.4 compared with 2.0 per 100,000 population.

In 1990, 67.3% of all suicides among teenagers aged 15–19 were the result of firearms. Since 1985 the overall rate of suicide for teenagers by firearms increased from 6.0 to 7.5

per 100,000. The group of teenagers with the largest percent increase was African-American males; however, white male teenagers (13.5 per 100,000) had a higher firearm suicide rate in 1990 compared with African-American males (8.8 per 100,000). During this same time period, the rate of suicide not involving firearms decreased for both African-American and white males and females.

Weapons in Schools

Schools are grappling with the problem of protecting children and school staff from the violence surrounding them. Episodes of violence, particularly gun violence, are increasing in schools and violent attacks involving even elementary school children appear to be on the increase. Thus, gun violence has become a major concern for schools across the nation—a concern that is no longer limited to large cities, but extends to smaller cities and rural areas.

School security and law enforcement officials estimate that four of every five firearms that are carried into schools come from the students' homes; they bring one of their parents' firearms for "show and tell" with friends. Law enforcement officials also note that firearms are easily accessible by other means. They are readily borrowed from friends, bought by proxy, stolen, or even rented. On the street, guns can be purchased for as little as $25. . . .

When weapons are carried into schools, especially guns, the potential for a violent episode is heightened and, in recent years, there have been far too many violent episodes involving weapons on school campuses that have led to tragedy. Preventing violence calls for school policies that provide for school environments that are free from violence for students, staff, and others on school premises. For some school systems this may mean providing such controls as locker searches, weapons searches, hiring police to patrol school premises, allowing students to wear only see-through backpacks, and possibly providing metal detectors upon entry. Some school systems have even created separate alternative schools for young people with a history of violent and abusive behavior. While this option is attracting attention, it is also controversial.

A study by the American School Board revealed that 50% of school districts conduct locker searches, 36% conduct search and seizure activities, 36% maintain security personnel in schools, 31% have gunfree school zones, and 15% have metal detectors. Approximately one-fourth of large urban school districts in the United States use metal detectors to help reduce weapon-carrying in schools. According to the Centers for Disease Control, these detectors may help reduce, but do not eliminate, weapon-carrying in schools and to and from schools. Students who attended schools with metal detector programs were as likely as those attending schools without metal detectors to carry weapons elsewhere, but were less likely to have carried a weapon inside the school building or going to and from school. Decreases in school-related weapon-carrying were due to decreases in the carrying of both knives and handguns. The presence of metal detectors had no apparent effect on the prevalence of threats and physical fights inside the school, to and from school, or anywhere else.

Security measures and equipment are expensive; walk-through metal detectors can cost up to $10,000 each and X-ray equipment designed to detect weapons in book bags can cost as much as $17,000. Hiring security personnel is also expensive. Despite these measures, students are known to have successfully carried weapons into schools, usually by sneaking them through windows or unguarded entrances, much to the frustration of many school administrators. Some school districts are reluctant to implement new security measures, particularly metal detectors, because they fear it may open them up to lawsuits.

The Need for Cooperative Action

It is obvious that schools alone cannot be totally effective in controlling availability of weapons. Controlling access will require the cooperation of many individuals and institutions. The New York Academy of Medicine has proposed the following:

1. Implementing a national licensure system for firearm possession;

2. Limiting the manufacture, sale, and distribution of military-style assault weapons;

3. Increasing the tax on firearms and ammunition;

4. Tightening federal licensing requirements for gun dealers;

5. Limiting the number of guns an individual can buy;

6. Implementing a gun return program;

7. Implementing a firearm fatality and injury reporting system; and

8. Educating the public to the dangers of guns and the need for national regulation.

*"The notion that the mere availability of
guns . . . can cause a perfectly normal,
happy kid to suddenly be transformed into
a heartless killer . . . is absurd."*

Guns Are Not the Cause of Youth Violence

Keith G. Benton

In the following viewpoint, therapist Keith G. Benton contends that violence among youths is a result of single parenting, poverty, and abuse, not the easy availability of guns. For instance, Benton maintains that children who live in single-parent, poverty-stricken households are at increased risk for learning and behavioral disorders and often grow into troubled, violent youths. Therefore, he claims that emphasizing gun control is an inadequate solution to reduce youth violence. Benton is a firearms enthusiast and former law enforcement officer.

As you read, consider the following questions:
1. How does the author describe the media's response to youth gun violence?
2. According to Benton, what are a child's Golden Years?
3. In the author's opinion, how does attachment disorder contribute to violence among children?

From "Kids and Violence: No Easy Answers," by Keith G. Benton, *Handguns*, May 2000. Copyright © 2000 by Petersen Publishing Company. Reprinted with permission.

"**K**ids and guns. Once more, a child has found easy access to a handgun, and the results are predictably tragic. A community is in mourning, and everyone is asking 'Why?'"

So goes the media mantra we have all heard far too many times in recent years. We are then buffeted with week after week of so-called "in-depth reporting." The cameras stare mercilessly at the faces of agonizing adults and sobbing, bewildered teens, as though we must all be taught exactly what grief looks like.

Then, when every maudlin moment has been drawn out to its maximum, heart-wrenching climax, a somber reporter faces the lens and asks, "Isn't it finally time to do away with these vile instruments of destruction, these guns, that have caused so much sorrow and tragedy?"

Not a Mystery

It all sounds so simple, so profound. Complex problems seldom have simple solutions, though, and this one is no exception.

We do not live in the same nation we did 40 or 50 years ago. We are not the same people because we do not act or think as we did then. We have become a society in which relationships are as disposable as Dixie cups, and the intact family is the exception rather than the norm.

The divorce rate remains pretty steady at about one-half, but the marriage rate has dropped more than 40 percent since the '60s. Those figures reflect the trend toward casual mating and away from establishing families. One in every three live births in this country now is to a single mother; and in many inner city areas, that rate is more than doubled. First-born illegitimacy tops 40 percent, nationwide.

Of course, we must not make any sort of value judgement about this trend (that is also part of what we have become), but the facts are undeniable. The best predictor of poverty is single parenthood, and the best predictor of a learning or behavior disorder is low socioeconomic status. Is that a mystery? It's really not.

The first four years of a child's life are sometimes referred to as "The Golden Years." That is because so much is learned and absorbed by the child during that time period. A newborn comes into the world basically clueless, equipped with only a few defensive reflexes. A need for personal, one-on-one care and affection is so hard-wired into the infant, though, that a lack of it can result in the child failing to thrive. At about four to five months, the infant's brain goes through what is called the cortical shift, volitional movement and cognitive functioning cut in, and the learning curve takes off like a rocket.

By the end of the first year, some very definite attitudes have been established. Developmental psychologist Erik Erikson's Stage Theory tells us that a one-year-old has already established whether his or her world is a place where people can be trusted. Mother is the primary figure. If the child's relationship with her is predictable and steady, the child sees the world as a good place. There is a sense of trust and security. If the child's life is unpredictable and chaotic, however, a sense of mistrust, anxiety and insecurity results. Repairs are difficult, and sometimes impossible.

Single parenting and poverty are driving the demand for more and more day care for children. That institutional, out-of-home care can begin as early as six weeks of age. The infants, toddlers and preschoolers that might be home with Mom, learning to feel secure, to speak and reason, to socialize appropriately and to trust and be trusted, are thrown in with a gaggle of peers. For eight to 12 hours a day, these tender little human beings in their Golden Years have one adult caretaker for every eight to 10 children, and usually not even the same caretaker for very long. Day care typically pays its workers minimum wage, and the rate of attrition is high.

Children under five who spend most of their time one-on-one with caring adults learn to be functioning human beings. Children under five who spend most of their time with other children learn to be barbarians. But, sometimes those are the lucky ones. Kids who spend their Golden Years in day care at least have a minimum standard of care and, usually, protection from abuse. Home might be worse.

Wrecking Children

Normally, young children are learning basic skills of attachment and trust, conflict resolution, self-regulation, sharing and empathy for others in their homes. Constant emotional arousal, however, such as daily exposure to physical danger and threats of violence, activates stress hormones. The constant presence of these catecholamines retards the brain's normal functioning. Branching and attachment of axons and dendrites between neurons, a necessary part of the growing and learning process in a young brain, doesn't happen as it should. Consequently, these traumatized children do not learn important social skills. Instead, they enter the world with a mind-set of survival. They cannot regulate their own level of emotional arousal, and they hate and mistrust anyone who tries to get close to them.

Middle-American Violence

Amid the national panic over school violence in March 2001, an enraged father in the affluent Santa Cruz suburb of Soquel gunned down his wife, two young sons, and himself. That one shooting in one suburban house on one day claimed more lives than all school gunfire nationwide in the entire month. Nor was this unusual; 40 times more children and youths are murdered by parents every year than in even the worst year for school homicide (1992–93), and 100 times more than in the most recent school year (2000–01). That these day-to-day middle-American massacres in virtually every adult institution bring little press and zero political deploring of our "culture of violence" leaves little justification for the trembling moral outrage that the schools serving 50 million Americans daily also are not immune. In bitter truth, it would be astounding if shootings never took place in American schools; the mystery is that they're so few.

Mike Males, *Bad Subjects*, April 11, 2001.

Children suffering from this "Attachment Disorder" typically have a compulsion to control everyone around them. They feel that no one can be trusted. Normal methods of discipline are useless, producing only aggression or defiance. They can be charming and manipulative, but they lack empathy and regard for others. Minimal arousal provokes instant violence. Even when caught in the act, they will lie, and there is little evidence of guilt or remorse for any harm they have done.

Imagine the ultimate nightmare. We produce this genera-

103

tion of frightened, distrustful, violent, unsocialized children. They have passed their fourth year, so the "gold" has all been spent, and any remedy has become double-tough. We then take them in groups of 30 or so, put them all in a room together and send some poor, benighted adult in to educate them! If you haven't visited a public classroom lately, you may think this scenario is a gross exaggeration. Across our nation, though, teachers are typically spending 50 to 90 percent of their classroom time just trying to maintain order! Attention deficit and hyperactivity diagnoses have become so common that, by 1996, America's school children were consuming 90 percent of the Ritalin produced in the world. Ten to 12 percent of the male students in our public schools take this addictive prescription medication to control their behaviors.

Working with these troubled kids and their caretakers, as I do every day, presents a very realistic perspective on just where youth violence originates. The notion that the mere availability of guns within a society can cause a perfectly normal, happy kid to suddenly be transformed into a heartless killer is not just farfetched, it is absurd. Violence comes from the rage and despair inside of kids, not some inanimate object. Adults that are supposed to be loving and nurturing have no time for them, and they're mad, really mad. The "Me generation" has gone to seed, and many, many children have paid the price for it. Now, we are all paying.

Some would still say, though, "Isn't it worth it, to save even one life, to do away with the guns? What is the value of your 'right' to own a gun, compared to the life of just one child? Shouldn't you be willing to give up your rights?"

That appeal might be very strong from a purely emotional perspective, but the answer is no! Of course, the death of any child is a tragedy beyond words, but trying to trade liberty for safety is a fool's proposition. We could turn the whole country into a Police State, one huge minimum security prison, and still not be safe.

A Level of Technology

Firearms merely represent a level of technology. They come from metallurgy, chemistry and know-how. They have been manufactured around the world for centuries, in modern factories and in mud huts. As long as people want them, they will get them. Outlaw them, and you simply create a new class of contraband. We already have lots of experience with that, don't we?

We must have surely proven by now that new legislation and more government spending is not the answer to our social problems with youth violence, or just about anything else. Instead, we must go back to that lowest common denominator of society, the individual. Change comes from inside people, one at a time, and anyone can help. Find a kid who is hurting, and lend a hand. It's slow and difficult, but sometimes it works.

"Bullying, often dismissed as a normal part of growing up, is a real problem in our nation's schools."

Bullying Among Youths Is a Serious Problem

Sue Smith-Heavenrich

Sue Smith-Heavenrich is a contributor to *Home Education Magazine*, a periodical that focuses on homeschooling. In the following viewpoint, Smith-Heavenrich claims that bullying is a long-ignored problem in America's schools. She contends that physical and verbal abuse can devastate some victims, many of whom resort to violence and suicide. Smith-Heavenrich concludes that schools need to do a better job of identifying bullies and intervening when bullying occurs.

As you read, consider the following questions:
1. How does the author support her view that American society openly tolerates violence?
2. In Smith-Heavenrich's view, what problems do many bullies face later in life?
3. What does the author suggest to help stop bullying in schools?

From "Kids Hurting Kids: Bullies in the Schoolyard," by Sue Smith-Heavenrich, *Mothering*, May/June 2001. Copyright © 2001 by Mothering Magazine. Reprinted with permission.

Bullying, often dismissed as a normal part of growing up, is a real problem in our nation's schools, according to the National School Safety Center. One out of every four schoolchildren endures taunting, teasing, pushing, and shoving daily from schoolyard bullies. More than 43 percent of middle- and high-school students avoid using school bathrooms for fear of being harassed or assaulted. Old-fashioned schoolyard hazing has escalated to instances of extortion, emotional terrorism, and kids toting guns to school.

A Culture of Competition and Dominance

Bullying exists in every Western or Westernized culture, from Finland and Australia to Japan and China. Three million bullying incidents are reported each year in the US alone, and over 160,000 children miss school each day for fear of being bullied. In Japan, bullying is called ijime. In 1993, just months before three suicides pushed ijime into the headlines, there were over 21,500 reported incidents of schoolyard bullying.

Many who flee urban streets to escape the culture of violence learn too late that bullying is more common in rural areas than in the cities. Researchers who surveyed hundreds of children living in the rural American Midwest found that 90 percent of middle school students and 66 percent of high school students reported having been bullied during their school careers.

Living in a culture that encourages competition and dominance, most Americans do not take bullying seriously. The problem, says University of California, Los Angeles Adjunct Associate Professor of Psychology Jaana Juvonen, is that ridicule and intimidation have become acceptable. Her studies indicate that starting in middle school, bullies are considered "cool," while their victims are rejected from the social milieu.

It is estimated that more than 90 percent of all incidents of school violence begin with verbal conflicts, which escalate to profanities and then to fists or worse. Our culture has a great degree of tolerance for violence as a solution to problems. Just stroll through the local toy store; you'll find star destroyers, robots that shred their enemies, and even dolls dressed in black trench coats, wearing ski masks and toting guns. It should come as no surprise, then, that the US ranks along with England, Ireland, and Canada as having more bullies per capita than just about anywhere else in the world.

Meet the Bullies

A bully is someone who verbally or physically picks on others. A school bully might push you out of your seat, kick you when your back is turned, demand lunch money, threaten or insult you, call you names, or make jokes about you. A bully might give you dirty looks and spread rumors about you.

In addition to physical violence, threats, and name-calling are behaviors that qualify as emotional bullying. Excluding a child from a group or tormenting, ridiculing, and humiliating someone are kinds of emotional violence. Bullying can be racist in nature, with slurs, taunts, graffiti, and gestures. It can be sexual, with one child making abusive comments or pushing unwanted physical contact on another.

Bullies try to shame and intimidate their victims and make them feel inadequate. Some bullies are active and aggressive; others are reserved and manipulative, relying on smooth talk and lies. Bullying is not gender specific; it is estimated that 25 percent of bullies are females. Regardless of how big they are or what they look like, all bullies want power and have difficulty seeing things from another person's perspective. Simply put, bullies use other people to get what they want. Researchers are now finding out that bullies are different from other children. Their aggression begins at an early age, and they tend to attribute hostile intentions to others. They perceive provocation where none exists and set out to exact revenge. Eventually they come to believe that aggression is their best solution to conflicts.

Formerly it was accepted that bullying was rooted in low self-esteem. Recent research by UCLA's Juvonen and others reveals, however, that bullies tend to regard themselves in a positive light. Up to about sixth grade they are fairly popular, but as they get older their popularity wanes. By the time they're in high school, they tend to hang out with others like themselves: self-styled tough guys who may get what they want but are not well liked.

The person most hurt by bullying is often not the victim but the bully. The bully's behavior interferes with learning and friendships, and later on with work, relationships, income, and mental health. Children who bully tend to turn into antisocial adults and are more likely to commit crimes, batter spouses, and abuse their children. One study shows that 60 percent of boys who were bullies in middle school had at least one court conviction by the age of 24.

One researcher followed the lives of 518 individuals from the age of eight to about 50. Those children who were labeled as bullies went on to receive more driving citations and court convictions and showed higher rates of alcoholism and antisocial personality disorders. Though their intelligence level in the early grades was on a par with that of other children, by the time they were 19, their aggressive behavior interfered with developing intellectual skills. In high school, these were the children who experimented more with sex, drugs, and alcohol and had higher dropout rates.

About one third of bullies are themselves victims of bullying, and a recent study shows that these children have a higher risk of depression and suicidal thoughts than other children. Clearly, being a bully can be hazardous to your health.

The Victims

It is not so much the nature of the harassment, whether verbal or physical, but the extent of the bullying that harms a child. Children who are chronically targeted are likely to become increasingly withdrawn from their peers and suffer increased risk of depression and suicidal thoughts. Some actually end up killing themselves.

Nathan Feris, a seventh-grade student at Dekalb (Missouri) High School, put up with four years of teasing and taunting. He was called "chubby" and "the walking dictionary." One day in March 1987, he brought a gun to school, fatally shot another student, then took his own life. Six years later Curtis Taylor, an eighth-grade honors student from Burlington, Iowa, ended his life. He had been bullied for three years, enduring name-calling, constant tripping and shoving, and vandalism to his bicycle. In 1994, 15-year-old Brian Head walked into his classroom in Woodstock, Georgia, and shot himself. Quiet and overweight, he had been teased and bullied until he could not put up with it anymore.

When Your Child Is the Victim

The best way to protect your children is to foster their confidence and independence. You must also be willing to take action when needed. First and foremost, listen to your children. Ask them about school, social events, playtime, and sports practice. Children who are victimized by bullies may feel ashamed and too embarrassed to tell anyone, so listen to the petty gripes they bring up.

Some children don't reveal much through conversation, but other signs might alert you to the fact that all is not well. They might be afraid of walking home from school or beg for a ride instead of taking the bus. They might become withdrawn, distressed, or anxious, or come home with clothes torn and books destroyed. They may ask for extra lunch money because they are paying someone off; they may cry themselves to sleep at night.

Playful or Damaging

People Weekly: Can teasing ever be good for kids socially, as some suggest?

Psychologist Dorothy Esplelage: It's not so simple, as all teasing hurts. Teasing can start out as playful and end up being damaging. Victims of teasing are hurting and often don't have friends. Moreover, there is strong evidence that bullying can escalate into physical aggression. A report done by the Secret Service, looking at all school shootings since 1940, found only one constant: The majority of the teenage shooters had been victimized.

People Weekly, February 5, 2001.

If you think your child is being picked on, take the time to gently draw his fears out in conversation. If he mentions bullying, take his complaints seriously. First, convince him that it is not his fault, that the bully's behavior is the source of the problem. Then give him the tools to deal with the bully. Telling a child either to ignore a bully or to fight back is not the solution. Rather, we need to help our children learn to be assertive—to stand up for themselves in a nonviolent manner and have the confidence to seek help when they need it. We need to encourage action and discourage violence.

If your child is the quiet sort of victim, encourage him to express his feelings. Help him learn skills to manage his anxiety. Teach him some basic social skills: what to say and how to say it. If your child is the sort who eggs on bullies and picks unnecessary battles, teach her to "stop and think." Help her to learn more appropriate ways of expressing anger and encourage her participation in cooperative group activities.

Working together, develop some protective strategies your child can use, a sort of "bully-proof armor." In addition, teach your child to stay away from kids with bullying behavior. You may even want to enroll him or her in a martial arts school.

If your child is being bullied, it is appropriate to call the school or organization where it is happening. You should keep a record of incidents, noting dates and details. And, though you may be tempted to call the bully's parents, do not do so. Instead, try to meet the parents in a neutral environment, perhaps a classroom with a teacher or counselor present, so you can focus on solving the problem instead of blaming each other.

Patience is essential, because bullying problems are not resolved overnight. Even as we help our children develop bully-busting strategies, we must also help them strengthen talents and skills that improve their self-esteem, such as music, sports, art, math—whatever your child has a passion for and is good at. We may need to help our children develop new friendships as well as strengthen the friendships they already have. Remember, children with friends are less likely to be targets of bullies.

When Your Child Is the Bully

The last thing you want to hear is that your child is a bully. Although your normal response is to be defensive, stop for a moment, take a few deep breaths, and defuse the situation. Say something like this: "Instead of labeling my child, please tell me what happened." Then make yourself listen. Remind yourself that this discussion is ultimately about your child's well-being, even though it may not seem so at the moment. If your

111

child is a bully, look for what is going on in her life to make her act this way. In talking with your child, do not blame her, and don't get pulled into a discussion about what happened or why. Instead, let her know that bullying is not acceptable in your family or in society. Offer your assistance. Ask her, "How can I help you with this? Who can you go see in school if you find yourself getting into this situation again?" Once you understand her feelings, you can teach her new ways of behaving. You can say, "If you are feeling frustrated, angry, or aggressive, here are some things you can do." Together, you can make a list and tape it to her wall. A particularly helpful activity may be to ask your child to "walk a mile" in the victim's shoes. Because bullies have trouble empathizing with their victims, it is important to discuss how it feels to be bullied.

How do you discourage a child from acting like a bully in the first place? It begins at home. Children who are treated with respect by their parents are less likely to become bullies. Never bully your children, either physically or verbally. Parents who frequently criticize their children, demand unquestioning obedience, or use spanking as punishment are sending the message that anger and intimidation are useful ways of getting what you want. Ridiculing kids, yelling at them, or ignoring them when they misbehave aren't helpful models of behavior either. Instead, use nonphysical discipline measures that are enforced consistently.

Parents who are overly permissive, who give in to obnoxious or demanding children, are letting them know that bullying pays off. Instead, teach the art of negotiation early on and help your children learn how to mediate their own disputes.

School Intervention

According to students, schools respond inadequately, if at all, to reported incidents of bullying. When Frank Barone, principal of Amsterdam High School in Amsterdam, New York, asked hundreds of eighth graders if they had ever been bullied, more than half (58.8 percent) responded in the affirmative. Yet when he asked their teachers how many students had been bullied, they put the figure at 16 percent. Clearly, adults don't recognize the extent of bullying that children face every day.

One researcher taped 52 hours of playground activity at a midsize Toronto school. She documented over 400 episodes of bullying—an average of one every seven minutes—yet teachers intervened in only one out of every 25 episodes. Another survey showed that 71 percent of teachers stayed out of or ignored incidents of teasing and bullying.

The attitudes and behaviors of teachers and school staff strongly determine the extent to which bullying manifests itself in school and on the playground. Where bullying is tolerated, it flourishes. Teachers have a tremendous amount of power to stop bullying behavior in their own classrooms by leading discussions in class. Together, students and their teacher can define bullying as unacceptable behavior, establish rules against it, and develop action plans so that students know what to do when they observe a bullying incident.

Teachers and other adults need to take immediate action when bullying does occur. They can confront bullies in private and notify the parents of both victims and bullies. Most of all, teachers can demand and model behavior grounded in respect and dignity. I've seen this work in classrooms where the teachers and students do not tolerate rude and aggressive behavior. The students feel safe, and they're excited about learning.

While individual teachers can teach tolerance, a better solution is to involve everyone in a schoolwide intervention program. Changing the school culture is more effective than focusing on individuals who misbehave. The best programs include both prevention and intervention. Where such programs have been implemented, the results are dramatic: bullying has decreased by up to 50 percent. Other benefits include reductions in truancy, vandalism, and fighting; improved classroom discipline; a more positive attitude toward schoolwork; and an increased satisfaction with school life among students.

McCormick Middle School, in South Carolina, adopted a program that set clear sanctions for bullies and provided counseling for both bullies and their victims. A year later, the number of students being bullied had dropped from 50 to 22 percent. Within the last three years, schools across the nation (indeed, worldwide) have been developing and implementing "bully-proofing" programs, some with snappy titles, such as "Expect Respect" or "Respect and Protect." These programs typically incorporate development of rules, discussions, role-playing, and other consciousness-raising activities into their daily routine. Some, like the one at Willow Creek Elementary School in Englewood, Colorado, depend upon the active efforts of the 80 percent of the children who are neither bullies nor victims to put a stop to the bullying.

Whatever the program, the key to success is having parents, educators, and community members work together to create a climate that clearly communicates a moral code in which cruelty is neither tolerated nor ignored.

*"There's reason to believe our bullying
'crisis' is exaggerated."*

The Extent of Bullying Is Exaggerated

Benjamin Soskis

In the following viewpoint, Benjamin Soskis refutes the
claim that bullying is a serious problem facing today's youth.
He asserts that studies reporting a high incidence of bullying among youths are flawed because they define bullying
too broadly. He warns that aggressive antibullying efforts
may vilify normal adolescent behavior and prevent children
from learning how to cope with social injuries that are simply a part of growing up. Soskis is a reporter for the *New Republic*, a periodical that examines political and social issues.

As you read, consider the following questions:

1. What types of adolescent behavior does Soskis consider
   normal?
2. In the author's opinion, what are the potential harms of
   zero-tolerance antibullying programs?
3. What does Soskis suggest to reduce bullying in schools?

Pity the poor bully. For decades he flourished, thanks to a national consensus that boys would be boys and a little roughhousing couldn't hurt. We indulged the noogie, winked at the charley horse, and thought it sort of funny when the high school tough crammed the band geek into the locker. Poking, taunting, name-calling—at least in modest doses—were considered a normal, if sometimes trying, part of adolescent development. One gave up one's lunch money not only in fear, but with a certain deference to the rules of the game.

"Onerous Culture of Bullying"

No longer. If the bully was once an accepted part of a basically healthy educational environment, he is now the embodiment of a youth culture so cruel that it leads persecuted children to kill. "Think back to third grade, sixth grade, ninth grade," intoned the *San Diego Union-Tribune*. "Maybe you were too short, too thin, too fat, too tall, too dumb, too smart. Too . . . whatever 'they' decided. They who tripped you, mocked you, grabbed your lunch. Stole your dignity, your confidence, your spirit." In March 2001, the *Los Angeles Times* spoke of bullies as a national pestilence: "If we could only round them up and herd them into detention, then haul their parents in for counseling, maybe we could isolate the menace of bullies in our midst." That same month, the Henry J. Kaiser Family Foundation released a survey showing that bullying has become schoolchildren's primary concern, surpassing drugs and discrimination. Attorney General John Ashcroft has lamented our "onerous culture of bullying." State legislatures in Georgia, New Hampshire, and Vermont have passed laws cracking down on it. And, in May 2001, the much-publicized release by the National Institute of Child Health and Human Development (NICHD) of a massive study of bullying seemed to confirm our worst fears: Of the more than 15,000 students surveyed in grades six through ten, a full 30 percent said they had been involved in bullying, either as victims or as perpetrators; 17.2 percent said it happened at least once a week.

This sudden national outcry against bullying has its roots in the spate of school shootings in recent years—in Jonesboro, Arkansas, Littleton, Colorado, Santee, California, and so on—several of which were conducted by students tormented by long-term harassment. And the outcry is, in many ways, a promising development—a cousin of our increased awareness of sexual harassment, bigotry, and other offenses. But, like many social movements born of tragedy, the anti-bullying movement has been characterized by widespread overreaction. Schools have outlawed dodgeball because it encourages bullies. They've cracked down on offenses as minor as a menacing look or a nasty gesture—because, as one California school district argued, these affronts "can be precursors to bigger conflicts." Every school is seen as a potential Columbine, every disgruntled student a potential Andy Williams.[1]

Distinguishing Tragedies and Petty Cruelties

In reality, there's reason to believe our bullying "crisis" is exaggerated—that, in the wake of Columbine, we're losing the capacity to distinguish between the imponderable tragedy of a school shooting and the petty, everyday cruelties that inevitably accompany adolescence. What's more, in our overwrought efforts to stamp out those mundane cruelties, we may actually end up making them worse.

Any discussion of bullying is complicated by the fact that, because there has been so little research on the subject until recently, it's difficult to know whether it's getting worse. But the perception that schools are becoming increasingly brutal is undermined by the fact that, according to a number of major indexes, youth violence is declining. The Justice Policy Institute reports that youth crime is at its lowest level in a quarter-century; the number of violent deaths occurring in or near school has decreased nearly 70 percent since 1992, from 55 to 16 per year. "To the extent that there is any trend at all, it is certainly not up," says the institute's director, Vincent Schiraldi. William Modzeleski, director of the Safe and Drug-Free Schools Program at the Department of Education, agrees, noting that schools are among the safest places for our kids to be.

1. In April 1999, Columbine High School in Littleton, Colorado, was the location of the most deadly school shooting in the United States. In March 2001, Williams was the perpetrator of a deadly school shooting in Santee, California.

How does this square with the recent studies that find widespread bullying in schools? It's basically a matter of definition —and the anti-bullying movement has broadened that definition beyond physical violence, threats, and taunting to include all potentially hurtful social interactions. The Michigan Education Association, for example, defines bullying to include spreading rumors and social exclusion—so refusing to include a klutz in a recess basketball game is a form of persecution. Ronald Stephens, executive director of the National School Safety Center and a leading proponent of anti-bullying programs, argues that "psychological intimidation can be as damaging as physical assaults." Therefore, he recommends that "hard looks" and "stare downs" be added to the actionable offenses in student codes of conduct. In May 2000, the state of New Hampshire enacted a law defining bullying as "conduct which subjects a pupil to insults, taunts or challenges, whether verbal or physical in nature, which are likely to intimidate or provoke a violent or disorderly response," and required schools to report all such incidents to the superintendent. But, as the chairman of one county school board complained, "What they define as bullying, it basically ends up being almost anything." The situation is particularly complex for girls, who, researchers agree, torment each other through subtler, less physical methods of "relational aggression," such as gossip or threats to withdraw friendship if certain conditions are not met.

Lost in the Furor

Even the vaunted NICHD survey illustrates the problem. Although it tried admirably to differentiate among particular forms of bullying, these distinctions were lost in the furor about the overall statistics. According to Tonja Nansel, the study's lead author, those overall numbers were based on the following definition: "We say a student is being bullied when another student, or group of students, say or do nasty or unpleasant things to him or her. It is also bullying when a student is teased repeatedly in a way he or she doesn't like, but it is not bullying when two students of the same strength quarrel or fight." Among the respondents, 10.6 percent said they had been bullied, 13 percent said they'd acted as bullies, and 6.3 percent said they'd been both bullies and bullied. But buried within the study's broad definition of bullying were numbers that mediate any sense of crisis: Just over half of those who'd been bullied—or about 9 percent of the total sample—said the bullying included a physical component, such as "hitting, slapping, or pushing." And of those bullied, only about 15 percent—a total of one student in a class of 40—said he or she was subjected to physical bullying once a week or more.

Defining Bullying Broadly

By defining bullying so broadly, the anti-bullying movement risks pathologizing behaviors that, however unpleasant, are in some sense normal parts of growing up and learning how to interact in the world. And this may not be in the long-term interest of either the bullies or the bullied. For the latter, zero-tolerance anti-bullying programs could leave them unprepared to assimilate the often unpleasant realities of social interaction without conceiving all hostility or peer rejection as traumatic. It's a similar danger to one already confronted by the self-esteem movement, a close relative of the anti-bullying effort. Initially, social scientists believed low self-esteem was often at the root of violent behavior. But, in recent years, a very different analysis has emerged: that unrealistically high self-esteem can lead to violence when challenged by negative feedback. Similarly, with bullying—though it is undoubtedly true that, for too long, parents and teachers failed to recognize the psychic trauma a child could experience from peer rejection—we can overcompensate if we do not train children to deal with the social slights that accompany adult life. In both cases, the danger is that, by trying to insulate children from harsh realities, we leave them more vulnerable and potentially more hostile when those realities inevitably intrude.

Anti-bullying researchers answer this challenge by arguing that, in fact, adults are never asked to tolerate the types of abuse we condone on the playground. According to Debra Pepler, a child psychologist at York University in Toronto, "[A]lthough there may be people in my work environment who I wouldn't want to take home for dinner on

Friday night, I don't tell them they can't sit beside me in a staff room, I don't say they can't be on a committee or they can't come to a meeting with me. Because as adults, we come to recognize and live with differences and we learn to live with relationships that don't need to be close friendships." But as adults, we do not stop excluding others or gossiping about them; we simply grow more adept at cloaking and interpreting the signals we send. There are plenty of ways one adult can humiliate and ridicule another in the workplace without calling him "Fatso." School is an opportunity to teach what forms of behavior should never be tolerated and what forms inevitably must be. So, as with a baby who, in the moment after a fall, looks to his mother for a cue for his response, it is important to know when to rush up and coddle a child and when to laugh as if it were nothing.

Infringing on Free Speech?

In focusing on gossip, rumors, and verbal offenses, the crusade has the obvious potential to infringe on free speech at schools. Will comments like "I think Catholicism is wrong," or "I think homosexuality is a sin," be turned into anti-bullying offenses?

John Leo, *U.S. News & World Report*, May 21, 2001.

But aggressive anti-bullying efforts may pose an even greater risk for the bullies themselves, who are increasingly vilified. This is the ironic reversal at the movement's core: Though launched onto the national stage by acts of extreme school violence, it considers the perpetrators of that violence not as bullies but as the victims of bullies. The actions of the school shooters are explained through references to their upbringing, environment, and status as victims. The anti-bullying movement rarely labels them obnoxious or evil—even when they espouse racist or anti-Semitic views, seem to court peer antagonism, or relish the attention their violent outbursts bestow upon them. The bullies who theoretically drove them to violence, however, get no such free ride: They're simply unfeeling jerks, popular kids wanting to demonstrate their social dominance of the shy or awkward.

This is an unfortunate bias considering what we know

about the psychology of bullies, specifically that they're often not so far removed from those they torment. According to recent studies, the line between the bullies and the bullied is often blurred, and the most troubled children fall into both categories. According to Pepler, those children "have significant problems with anxiety and depression and what are called internalizing disorders, as well as with problems with aggression and delinquency." In a 1999 study of Finnish students, depression was just as common among the bullies as among the bullied, and the former were even more likely to contemplate suicide. Bullies have high rates of truancy and are likely to come from troubled families. According to a pioneer of bullying research, Norwegian psychologist Dan Olweus, though bullies are usually well-liked by their peers when they're young, when they enter high school, where physical aggression is less tolerated, they are often shunned and forced to socialize with other aggressive children.

Given this profile, it is deeply counterproductive to treat bullies the way some in the anti-bullying movement propose—by stigmatizing them as fundamentally alien from their innocent classmates. There are already accounts of anti-bullying programs ostracizing the more belligerent and unruly students in class, creating exactly the sort of exclusionary social dynamic the programs claim to combat—but this time, in an inversion that would make [philosopher Friedrich] Nietzsche cringe, with the meek on top. A parent of a second-grader in Casper, Wyoming, complained that her son became severely depressed when he was not voted into his class's Caring Community, a bully-proofing program in which students elect their peers based on whom they consider respectful and responsible. His mother called the program a "popularity contest" and told a local newspaper, "I've seen kids leaving the school crying because they didn't get into the Caring Community. You should see the devastation in their eyes."

The Student Body as a Whole

You would hope anti-bullying activists would try to help these students rather than demonize them. And some do. The best anti-bullying programs—the ones that have been shown, in the limited research to date, to genuinely reduce school violence—do not isolate particular children. Rather, they speak to the student body as a whole, encouraging peers and bystanders to intervene when they think it is appropriate and making sure students have particular adults they can talk to when they feel especially troubled. These programs have learned much from the lessons of Columbine and Santee— about heeding warning signs from the bullies and bullied alike without overreacting to everyday slights; about the importance of parents, teachers, and administrators not lumping children into simplistic binary categories; and, perhaps most crucially of all, about how to teach children to differentiate between the kind of social injury they must learn to endure and the kind that we, as a society, must ensure they never have to.

Periodical Bibliography

The following articles have been selected to supplement the diverse views presented in this chapter.

Allison Adato	"The Secret Lives of Teens: We Traveled the Country, Asking Adolescents 'What's on Your Mind?' The Answer: Plenty. Here Is What They Confided," *Life*, March 1, 1999.
Susan Brenna	"STRESSED OUT!" *New York Times Upfront*, January 3, 2001.
Brown University Child and Adolescent Behavior Letter	"Surgeon General: Youth Violence Epidemic Not Over," March 2001.
Julie Collins	"Virginity Lost and Found: When Infatuation Fades, Inexperienced Teens Can Be Appalled That They Were So Clueless," *America*, May 21, 2001.
Dennis D. Embry	"Why More Violent Young Offenders?" *Corrections Today*, December 2001.
Pearl Gaskins	"Teen Violence: Violent Behavior Peaks During Adolescence. As the Toll of Teen Violence Grows, Scientists Search for Reasons Why," *Scholastic Choices*, October 2001.
Doug Ireland	"Gay Teens Fight Back," *Nation*, January 3, 2000.
Linda Marsa	"The Dangerous Search for a Good Time," *Family Circle*, June 1, 1999.
Anna Mulrine	"Are Boys the Weaker Sex?" *U.S. News & World Report*, July 30, 2001.
David Oliver Relin	"Drug E-mergency," *Teen People*, March 15, 2001.
Randolph E. Schmidt	"Teen Smoking, Drug Use Falling," *San Diego Union-Tribune*, December 20, 2001.
Andrew Stuttaford	"De-Demonizing Rum: What's Wrong with Underage Drinking?" *National Review*, June 25, 2001.
Alan J. Zametkin, Marisa R. Alter, and Tamar Yemini	"Suicide in Teenagers: Assessment, Management, and Prevention," *JAMA*, December 26, 2001.

CHAPTER 3

What Values Do Young People Hold?

Chapter Preface

Many adults feel that young people lack basic values, such as honesty, proper work ethics, and responsibility. For example, a 1998 survey by the Barna Research Group (BRG), a marketing research firm, concluded that many adolescents believe that adults commonly hold them in low esteem. Teenaged respondents were asked to use adjectives to describe how adults view young people, and terms such as "lazy" (chosen by 84 percent), "rude" (74 percent), and "violent" (57 percent) frequently surfaced.

While BRG did not survey adults on their views of today's youth, Public Agenda, a policy analysis center, published "Kids These Days: What Americans Really Think About the Next Generation" in 1999. In this survey, 71 percent of two thousand adult respondents claimed that terms such as "lazy," "disrespectful," and "wild" described their first impressions of what young people are like today. In addition, only 14 percent stated that it was "very common" for adolescents to be friendly and helpful towards neighbors. Furthermore, 60 percent maintained that the failure of adolescents to learn values such as "respect," "honesty," and "responsibility" is a serious problem. Reiterating their views, Deborah Wadsworth, executive director of Public Agenda, insists that adults are "virtually riveted by the need to teach kids integrity, ethical behavior, respect, and civility."

However, many commentators believe that adults' negative views of young people are shaped by factors other than their actual behavior. For instance, some assert that the media focuses on violent behavior more than ever before and has affected adults' perception of youths. According to psychiatry professor Otto Kaak, "Adolescents who go on killing sprees—that gets widely covered. The media don't talk too much about the kid who got the scholarship." Other analysts insist that negative attitudes toward the next generation have always existed. Sociology professor Joanna Badagliacco claims that "every generation has thought the next generation had problems, and today the adults see the children as disrespectful, lazy, and living by different values."

Although many adults believe that today's teens are less

respectful and motivated than were teenagers of the past, many analysts point out that adults of every generation are critical of teenagers. In the following chapter, the authors discuss what values young people hold, how their values shape their behavior, and compare their values with those held by those from previous generations.

> "[Today's youth] may be a generation uniquely wired to stand—and sweat—for God."

Young People Hold Christian Values

Wendy Murray Zoba

Wendy Murray Zoba is a senior writer for *Christianity Today* and author of the book *Day of Reckoning: Columbine and the Search for America's Soul*. In the following viewpoint, Zoba contends that "Millennials"—youths who are coming of age at the start of the twenty-first century—look to Christianity for guidance. She suggests that the dramatic rise in the number of Christian youth mission trips shows that an increasing number of young people are genuinely interested in developing spiritually. Zoba claims that these trips help Christian youths reaffirm their faith while helping less fortunate people.

As you read, consider the following questions:

1. How does Zoba characterize the Millennials?
2. Why did Noah join the youth mission trip, according to Zoba?
3. In the author's view, what did the youths accomplish during their mission in Shell?

Excerpted from "Youth Has Special Powers," by Wendy Murray Zoba, *Christianity Today*, February 5, 2001. Copyright © 2001 by Christianity Today, Inc. Reprinted with permission.

If their rising interest in mission trips is any indication, the Millennials may be a generation uniquely wired to stand—and sweat—for God.

As a young man of 23, missionary Jim Elliot wrote in his journal, "For youth there is special wretchedness; for then the powers within conflict most bluntly with the powers without. Restraint is most galling, release most desired. To compensate for these, youth has special powers."

The so-called special "wretchedness" and "powers" of today's youth have been the subject of much of the cultural conversation recently. The string of school shootings over the past few years and other alarming trends (like anorexia and self-mutilation) have aroused national soul-searching and highlight the extremes, positive and negative, of the generation known as the Millennials. [The Millennials are the generation that follow Generation X, born between 1977 and 1995. Also known as Generation Y.]

Despite the troubling signals, there is still plenty of good news. "The unsung story of today's teenagers may be how religious they are," wrote John Leland in *Newsweek*. Indeed, in a *Newsweek* poll, 78 percent of teenagers said religion is important, and many gladly identified themselves as "spiritual," though few wanted to be labeled "religious." Christian pollster George Barna notes that two out of three teens strongly desire a personal relationship with God. The downside, according to Barna, is that fewer than half are excited about church, which has left many church leaders wondering how to reach this complicated and disparate cohort.

Trends and demographics are open to interpretation. But two characteristics are emerging as defining features of many Millennials: They are activists, and they long for God. One place where they and the church are coming together in a happy collaboration is the mission trip. This experience is becoming so prevalent in youth ministry that many high school pastors see it almost as a rite of passage.

"A youth mission trip offers a great opportunity for discipling," says Seth Barnes, executive director of Adventures in Missions (www.adventures.org), a Gainesville, Georgia–based ministry that sponsors and coordinates trips for youth groups around the country. Barnes says proper screening and training are essential because some teens go simply for the adventure or to get away from home. But assuming those checks are in place, he says the trip itself is an excellent tool for training a young person in the hard work of following Christ.

"It requires discipline, reaching out to others, and personal holiness," he says, all of which appeal to the activist and spiritual inclinations of the Millennials. The exponential rise in the number of trips reflects their interest in such an enterprise. Short-term mission trips numbered around 25,000 people in 1979. By 1989 that number had jumped to 120,000, and by 1995 to 200,000.

Many youth pastors believe mission trips are one way to call youth to a higher level of accountability and, says Barnes, "They are answering that call."

I observed the "phenomenon" up close the summer of 2000 when my husband Bob and I (and three other younger leaders) led a group of 12 teens to the jungles of Ecuador. One mission trip does not denote a trend for an entire generation. But it offers a window into the kind of gritty spirituality that animates many of today's teens.

Why They Went

The teens we took were suburban and white, and most had been raised in Christian homes. They were active in the senior-high youth program at College Church in Wheaton, Illinois, and each had a personal reason for making the trip.

Stephanie wanted to know she had "suffered to help someone." Rachel prayed that the trip would "restore humility" in her. Susanna didn't want to go at first but felt the Lord wanted her to do it. Nate said that God had recently shown him "the true horrors of what an eternal hell would be like" and so activated his otherwise passive faith.

Karen said she wanted the "chance to serve" because God had been showing her "how selfish and ungrateful" she was. Abby hoped for the opportunity to work with needy children. Noah wanted to "share the gospel and love with others." Stephen sensed a call to become a missionary pilot and wanted exposure to missions.

Kyle hoped it "would change how I view the way I live."

Tim wanted "to see the poverty and helplessness in the world." Our sons Ben and Jon, also team members, went because Jon wanted "to bring God glory," and Ben wanted "to be a servant like [Christ] was."

The team went to work with the missionary community serving HCJB World Radio, based in Quito (HCJB stands for "Heralding Christ Jesus' Blessings"). We were to drive east of Quito, to the outskirts of the jungle to work with the missionaries who lived in a town called Shell (named by the oil company; population 5,000). They ran a hospital sponsored by HCJB that served nationals and people from the jungle tribes. The original hospital there had been built in the 1950s by Nate Saint, one of the five missionaries who died in 1956 at the hands of the Auca Indians (today known as the Huaorani; pronounced War-dah-nee). Saint and the others had departed from Shell when they took their fateful trip into the jungle to meet the tribe. Saint had secured land in Shell and donated a portion to HCJB for that purpose. All five martyred men worked on the crew that built that first hospital. It had since been converted to the guesthouse where we stayed. The martyrs' black-and-white photos hung in the hallway. . . .

No Time for Blisters to Heal

Once in Shell, we reported to the maintenance area where missionary Alex Weir showed Bob the list of jobs he hoped we would accomplish that week. Bob shook his head and didn't think we could do it in the time we had. But the teens were up for the challenge. Alex divided us into teams: one crew painted the school library, another poured a new concrete sidewalk, and the crew I was on removed the dingy ceiling tiles from the north wing of the hospital with the plan to repaint and replace them all. . . .

At the end of the first day, spirits were high despite the blistered hands and tired muscles. Noah launched our evening devotions. "This morning I was reading in Nehemiah, and one of his prayers was that God would be his strength. God showed me the impact the Spirit has on your physical being," he said. "Paul commands us not to complain or grumble. We should make that our goal."

"I was reading Colossians today," said Jon. "In 3:23 we're commanded to work. It's not an option. We're commanded to be happy and cheerful when we work.". . .

The work got tougher day by day, and there was no time for blisters and muscles to heal. One crew lost half a day trying to pull one stubborn boulder from a ditch. Working around patients in stretchers or wheelchairs and hearing children cry was taking its toll on the ceiling-tile crew at the hospital. A baby with pneumonia, clinging to life, hacked with such struggle that each cough sounded like it would be her last. Sometimes nurses shushed us as we worked. A mouse ran across one ceiling tile as we pulled it out; another mouse lay dead on a different tile.

Many in our group contended with sickness; others were losing sleep from itching and burning bug bites. It rained constantly, which meant our clothes didn't dry when we hung them up. After a week's work, our "infirmities," as the apostle Paul calls them, were laid bare before one another. Noah and Tim hadn't done laundry all week, and their dirty clothes, strewn all over the floor of their room, stunk up the hallway. Some complained when we changed their work assignments; others maneuvered to be placed on a different crew. More than once I was ignored as I tried to relay pertinent instructions. We confronted tears, squabbles, jealousies, and hurt feelings—on top of fatigue, intestinal disorders, nausea, and raw nerves.

Praying for Patience

Still, we gathered every night for student-led devotions. Karen was scheduled to lead after one particularly grueling day, but first had to fight for her bag of Cheez-Its snatched by one of the guys. Then she opened with Scripture.

"This morning I was reading in Isaiah, and, well, this is what I read: 'Come, all you who are thirsty, come to the waters; and you who have no money, come, buy, and eat! . . . Seek the Lord while he may be found; call on him while he is near.'"

The group, sore and subdued, sat attentively while she read. After a stretch of silence, Stephen said, "I learned perseverance today. My arms hurt, and I did not feel like I could keep going. But I realized you just have to mix that next batch of cement, no matter what it takes."

"I prayed for patience with the ceiling tiles," said Tim.

"Trying to pull that boulder out made me think that it was like our sin," said Kyle. "It took a whole group of us working together to get it out and move it to where it could be forgotten."

See You at the Pole

"See You at the Pole" is a grassroots phenomenon that has obviously met a felt need and touched a raw nerve in American society, or at least the public school subculture of that society. [In "See You at the Pole," students meet at their school's flagpole to pray.]

The prayer movement is a student-initiated, student-led phenomenon of young people from the so-called "Millennial Generation," a group who seem to possess rich religious faith. Ministers and volunteers who have worked with young people for many years report that you cannot be around today's Christian young people for very long without noticing their particular spiritual intensity for personal and national spiritual renewal. Many baby boomers, baby busters, and Generation Xers will attest that there is a fervor and intensity in today's teenagers that their generations too often lacked.

Richard Land, www.beliefnet.com (no date).

Noah was sick but got out of bed to play guitar and lead the singing: "I lift my eyes unto the heavens; where does my help come from? My help comes from you, Maker of Heaven, Creator of the earth."

Sick and exhausted, the teens bobbed their heads as they sang and closed their eyes. The girls lifted their faces, and the guys folded their blistered hands. They sang past the quiet curfew at the guesthouse, but nobody complained. By the evening's end, everyone had forgiven Tim and Noah for stinking up the hallway—and Susanna ministered to them, and to us all, when she heroically did their laundry the next day.

40,000 Pounds of Cement

Stephanie led the [last devotion of the mission]. "This whole trip has been a really awesome demonstration of his love for us and it really, like, revived my spirits and stuff." She read a portion from C.S. Lewis's *Mere Christianity*: "Our moods change. . . . That is why daily prayers and religious reading and churchgoing are a necessary part of the Christian life. We have to be continually reminded of what we believe."

"We've all been changed here," Stephanie said. "We can't let our friends make us normal again. We can't forget it. It's our job to go back and share this awesome experience with everybody and remind them of what we've been reminded here this week."

They also reflected on the work accomplished that week. "For the record," Stephen said, "in the last week, the cement crew has mixed about 40,000 pounds of cement." We poured sidewalks, painted the school library and basketball court, put in a basketball hoop, dug a drainage ditch, built a carport, landscaped one side of the hospital, and replaced all of the ceiling tiles in one wing of the hospital. Alex crossed almost every job off his list. . . .

A Generation of Disciples

It is difficult to measure the true impact a mission trip has on the lives of young people. One layer of enthusiasm has to be peeled away by virtue of their being teens. But the "special powers" of youth, to which Elliot referred, shine bright in an experience like this. People have to die a lot of little deaths on a mission trip, forcing them to submit their individual wills to the greater purpose.

There were days that our teens did not want to work and didn't think they could lift another shovelful of dirt. But they pressed on, emboldened by their singing and a sense that the Holy Spirit was giving them new strength. The Ecuadorian foremen who oversaw their work used the Spanish words *santidad* and *servicio* to describe these youth: "holy" and "servants."

It is too soon to tell whether these virtues will play out over the long haul. But seeing the Millennials in our group using their limited Spanish to talk with people, running hut to hut with the Huaorani kids, crying and praying on their knees, and singing hymns when their flesh felt its weakest, gives me reason to hope.

After we returned from Ecuador, several youth from our town, including young people from our trip, organized a community event to reach their unchurched peers. They called it Power Jam. The young people themselves planned, prayed, and orchestrated the event with no adult input, doing everything from running the cotton-candy machine to leading the worship. Six hundred local youth showed up.

All of the youth who led the Power Jam had recently been on mission trips, observes Rod Van Solkema, who at the time was senior-high pastor at College Church. He adds, "They learned on those trips, 'If God can use me over there, why can't he use us over here?'"

A mission trip will not set the course for an entire generation. But, as it did with our group, it can help young people to see a God who is alive in his world—where trees climb upward to return God's glory to himself; where the Spirit builds up the physical being; where the sinful nature can be slaughtered with a song.

It's too soon to tell if the mission-trip trend is raising a generation of disciples. But it's a start.

> "[Christian] faith is a passing fancy of
> young people."

Young People Do Not Hold Christian Values

Barna Research Group

The Barna Research Group (BRG) is a marketing research company that analyzes Christianity in the context of cultural trends. In the following viewpoint, the BRG argues that the importance of Christian faith has diminished in the lives of today's youth. The organization claims that faith-related goals are not as important to youths as are goals related to strong relationships and lifestyle comforts. Furthermore, although more youths than adults are active in the church, the BRG concludes that teens who become involved in church activities are more interested in fostering friendships than developing spiritually.

As you read, consider the following questions:

1. How do religious goals rank among the national sample of youths studied by the BRG?
2. In George Barna's view, why is youths' desire to be portrayed as religious a contradiction?
3. What should the church do to earn the time and attention of teens, as stated by Barna?

If you want to understand the future, you have to understand those who will dictate the contours of the days to come. A new nationwide survey among teenagers, conducted by the Barna Research Group [which provides information and analysis of cultural trends and Christianity] reveals many exciting and encouraging changes that are likely to occur. But one shift that should trouble leaders in the Christian Church is the superficial relationship that most teens have with Christianity—and their plans to reduce their already minimal commitment to the Christian faith.

American teenagers are widely described as deeply religious individuals who have integrated their religious beliefs into their lifestyle and their thinking. This latest study among teens, however, suggests that faith is a passing fancy of young people—just one of many dimensions that they blend into a potpourri of perspectives, experiences, skills, and contexts toward arriving at their worldview and lifestyle. Neither their behavior nor their beliefs support the notions that they are deeply spiritual or truly committed to Christianity. Although their spirituality is more overt than that of their elders, teenagers are even less committed to Christianity than are the Baby Boomers.

Talk Is Cheap

While teens are well-known to spend more time discussing religious matters than do older people, that running commentary on spiritual matters has yet to translate to a deeper sense of commitment to spirituality. Even when asked to describe themselves, terms that reflect a religious bent are common, but no more so than is found among adults. For instance, less than two-thirds say that they are "religious" (64%). Only three out of every five call themselves "spiritual" (60%) and the same proportion say they are "committed Christians" (60%). These figures are equivalent to those among adults.

It is interesting to note that among those who deem themselves to be committed Christians, only half qualify as born again Christians, a categorization that includes having "made a personal commitment to Jesus Christ that is still important in [their] life today."

One way of measuring the significance of spirituality in their lives is to explore their goals for their future. When the national sample of teens was asked to rate the desirability of each of 19 outcomes, the spiritual outcomes included in the list were of moderate significance, at best. Highest among the three religious-oriented outcomes was "having a close, personal relationship with God," which ranked just eighth out of the nineteen possibilities. "Being deeply committed to the Christian faith" was in the bottom third of the future possibilities, ranked fourteenth. "Being personally active in a church" placed even lower, placing sixteenth. Overall, the highest-ranking options related to strong relationships and lifestyle comforts. Faith matters were substantially less compelling considerations.

In fact, although an overwhelming majority believes in God, just two out of three teens strongly desire having a personal relationship with Him. Similarly, although nearly nine out of ten teenagers believe that Jesus was real, and more than eight out of ten describe themselves as Christian, only half say they are very eager to be deeply committed to the Christian faith. Even fewer—just four out of ten—are excited about being active in a church.

Overt Commitments

Three key measures of faith further reveal the true nature of the spirituality of teens. Although four out of five say they are Christian, only one out of four (26%) also claims to be "absolutely committed to the Christian faith." That is only about half the percentage found among adults—and a strong indicator of the flagging depth of loyalty Americans have in relation to its dominant faith group.

Another measure is that of born again Christians. Survey respondents were classified as born again if they had made a personal commitment to Jesus Christ that is still important in their life and if they believed that after they die they will go to Heaven solely because they have confessed their sins and have accepted Jesus Christ as their savior. Using this classification method just one out of every three teens (33%) is born again. Amazingly, less than half of the born again teenagers (44%) said that they are absolutely committed to the Christian faith—yet another harbinger of trouble for the future Church.

Barna Research surveys consistently evaluate the percentage of individuals who are evangelicals. That group is based on people who meet a series of belief-based criteria. Presently, only 4% of U.S. teens fit the evangelical criteria—roughly the same as among adults (6%).

Privatisation of Faith

In the last quarter of the 20th century, we've witnessed the privatisation of the Christian faith. Beliefs and values have become individual matters; religion and ministry are confined to our "personal lives." The public arena has been left to TV executives, politicians, educators, scientists and economists—all purveyors of their own ideologies. This has left our society without positive moral direction and Christianity without significant witness and impact in the public arena. If Christianity is to make a difference among young people, it must publicly and assertively evangelize the next generations.

Roland Martinson, *GROUP Magazine*, 1993.

Perhaps the most deceptive factor is the high level of church-based involvement among today's teenagers. This study shows that teens continue to be more broadly involved in church-based activities than are adults. In a typical week, nearly six out of ten attend worship services; one out of three attend Sunday school; one out of three attend a youth group; and three out of ten participate in a small group, other than a Sunday school class or youth group meeting. In total, more than seven out of ten teens are engaged in some church-related effort in a typical week. That far exceeds the participation level among adults—and even among teenagers' parents!

But before these levels of involvement result in celebration, be warned about teens' plans for the future. When asked to estimate the likelihood that they will continue to participate in church life once they are living on their own, levels dip precipitously, to only about one out of every three teens. Placed in context, that stands as the lowest level of expected participation among teens recorded by Barna Research in more than a decade. If the projections pan out, this would signal a substantial decline in church attendance occurring before the close of this new decade.

What's Going On?

These statistics were collected as part of a larger study of teenagers, described in a new report by researcher [and president of BRG] George Barna entitled "Third Millennium Teens." Among the conclusions of the report is that teenagers are a study in contradictions. One of those is their simultaneous desire to be portrayed as religious people while they invest little of themselves in true spiritual pursuit. The research discovered that religious participation by teens is often motivated by relational opportunities rather than by the promise of spiritual development. The possibility of making and retaining friendships outstrips their commitment to deepening their faith. The relative lack of interest in maintaining church ties in the future reflects their experience with churches to date. Specifically, they do not perceive churches to be particularly helpful.

George Barna, who directed and analyzed the research, indicated that it is not too late to persuade teenagers to include the church in their future plans. "Most teens are desperately striving to determine a valid and compelling purpose for life. Most of them want to have influence and impact. The Church has an opportunity to address such matters and thus to position itself as a place of valuable insight and assistance." Barna stated that young people will give the Church a chance. "But to become an accepted partner in their maturation process, the Church must earn the time and attention of teens—and that means becoming a provider of value well before their high school graduation. The failure to do so virtually guarantees that the Church will continue to see massive dropout rates among college students, with relatively few of those young people returning to the church immediately after college."

| "*Public service and volunteer work are more popular [among young people] than ever.*"

Young People Are Interested in Politics

Rudy Kleysteuber

In the following viewpoint, Rudy Kleysteuber asserts that while voter turnout among young people has been declining, many youths are active in public service, volunteer work, and political support networks. Furthermore, he contends that numerous youths run for and hold political office. Kleysteuber is a staff reporter for the *Wall Street Journal*.

As you read, consider the following questions:

1. How does Jason Nastke describe today's youth?
2. According to Kleysteuber, where are youths' interests in politics especially visible?
3. To what factor does Brett Bruen attribute his loss in a primary election for city council?

S tephanie McLeod was elected to public office at the age of 20.

On Nov. 3, 1998, she won 16,251 votes and a seat on her county's nine-member Mosquito Control Board. "I went and spoke in public forums, and I had ads in the local newspapers," Ms. McLeod says. Her campaign slogan attracted instant attention: "Elect New Blood."

That doesn't fit the popular image of Generation X and Generation Y, who are known today for their political apathy: voter turnout is at a record low, and pop-culture attempts to boost participation have failed to incite widespread interest in politics. Age aside, voter turnout has been declining in general. But among 18-to-24-year-olds, turnout was down to 32% in 1996 from 50% in 1972, the first year all 18-year-olds could vote.

Youthful Attraction

Beneath an apathetic young electorate lies a trend of an entirely different nature, however. Public service and volunteer work are more popular than ever. And, like Ms. McLeod, some young people are even running for political office. "You have to look at my entire generation," says Jason Nastke, who in 1999 at age 19 was elected the mayor of Valatie, N.Y., a town of about 2,200 residents near Albany. "To say that they're not civic-minded is just crazy. They're the most educated generation we've seen. They care about the issues."

Evidence of the youthful attraction to politics is no more than a click away on the Internet, where new support networks such as the Young Politicians of America are getting stronger every day. "We have members who are 11 or 12," says YPA co-founder Christian Shelton, 18, who estimates his group has about 1,000 members. "The average age is probably around 18."

Based in California, the national organization provides an online forum for young people interested in politics. Mr. Shelton says most members of the Young Politicians of America are aiming for the same goal. "I can safely say that most of our members do aim to achieve political office as soon as possible."

Since he was old enough to play with G.I. Joe soldiers, Brett Bruen has always been an aspiring politician. Instead of waging military campaigns against each other, his pint-size plastic commandos faced off in political debates. "I divided my house up into districts and ran my G.I. Joes for office," Mr. Bruen says.

That might explain why in 1999 Mr. Bruen, at the age of 18, decided to run for city council in the student-dominated fifth district of Madison, Wis. The race pitted him against two other young candidates: a 19-year-old and a 33-year-old.

Changing the World Today

There are three fundamental ways in which youth are changing the world today. First, the way they participate socially and politically has vastly changed. . . . The way young men and women think of themselves as members of society and how they express their participation through various networks and associations is profoundly different from those of previous generations. For instance, youth have rejected political parties as an avenue of participation in the electoral process. Apathy toward Washington doesn't mean that youth just crumble up and die. All across the country, youth are banding together in diverse ways to change their communities and their lives. They are shifting their attention to other activities whereby they can really make a difference. It is likely to be close to home, in their own backyards . . . building housing for the homeless, working in soup kitchens, helping the elderly, advocating for youth, educating underprivileged kids, etc.

Matthew Moseley, *National Civic Review*, Summer/Fall 1995.

But Mr. Bruen experienced firsthand the nationwide trend of youthful voter apathy and lost in the primary. His time-honored campaigning tactics of shoe leather and telephone canvassing failed him, he says, because many of the students he reached didn't go to the polls. "One of the interesting or frustrating aspects of the race was the particularly low turnout in the student district," he says. Only 533 people voted—about a 10% turnout.

"The assumption that I made was that if you get out there and go door-to-door and talk to people, then they would in turn get out and vote," he says. "And that didn't end up happening."

Eric Zeemering, who won a seat on the Rockford, Mich.,

City Council in November 1999 at age 19, says he hopes that the involvement of young politicians will boost youth participation in politics.

"I think that as more people from my generation . . . form stronger connections to their communities, they'll become more involved in the political process," he says. "Because ultimately, the political process will impact the programs they work on and the causes they care about."

Despite his youth, Mr. Zeemering, now 20, got involved in politics years before running for office. He worked for a state representative, helped in a political campaign and is the campaign manager in a local race. But, more importantly, he says he has a fresh outlook on old issues.

"I'm young, I have a new perspective, and I have something to say that's not being said already," he says. "The key is really communicating to the public that we have something to offer." Adopting the age-old dictum that all politics is local, Mr. Zeemering focused on supporting fire and police services. "I think that police service is the most important thing a municipality provides to its residents," he says.

A Fresh Perspective

A fresh perspective is what Chris Tiedeman, 24, is offering in his bid for the Minnesota House of Representatives. His opponent, incumbent Bernie Lieder, was first elected in 1984 and is serving his eighth term in the Minnesota House. "As a 24-year-old running against a 77-year-old, age becomes a tremendous advantage for me," Mr. Tiedeman says. As for experience, he hopes his education and travel background can make up for his more-recent birthday. "To say that I lack experience would be a fruitless argument, and I don't expect to hear it, either," he says.

His opponent doesn't intend to raise it, either. "I don't think we should be involved in the experience issue, and I don't think he should be involved in the age issue," Mr. Lieder says.

Mr. Tiedeman says he plans to focus on voters of all ages, not just young ones. Other candidates say they hope their classmates will be their most loyal support. [Tiedeman lost the election.]

Bob Gienko, a 20-year-old student at Dartmouth College in New Hampshire, is running for the state's House of Representatives. "I hope to rally the support of my peers," Mr. Gienko says. "If we just go out and vote, we can have an impact."

Mr. Gienko also hopes to recruit his peers as volunteers, helping to canvass voters and be "foot soldiers on the ground." He faces serious obstacles rallying student support at the polls. New Hampshire's voter-registration laws don't permit college students to vote in the state without claiming full-time residence. "Because Dartmouth students are mostly out-of-state, a lot of candidates haven't focused on the college all that much," Mr. Gienko comments. "I'd like to see that change."

Rocking the Vote

Ms. McLeod, for her part, didn't need the student support. She estimates the average voter age in her district to be "well into the 50s." But that doesn't stop her from wanting to increase her generation's political participation.

"I would love to get in with MTV and get involved with 'Rock the Vote,'" Ms. McLeod says of the cable-TV network's campaign to recruit young voters. "It would be really neat to travel around and tell people how imperative it is to voice their opinion and not be so apathetic."

Ms. McLeod says she is considering a long-term political career. "I'm thinking I'm going to run for county commissioner, maybe in the year 2006."

"Young people aren't convinced that politics makes a difference in their lives."

Young People Are Not Interested in Politics

Alliance for Better Campaigns

The Alliance for Better Campaigns is a public interest group aimed at improving elections through campaign reform. In the following viewpoint, the Alliance for Better Campaigns argues that youths are not politically active and that voter turnouts among eligible voters between the ages of eighteen and twenty-four are very low. The alliance attributes low voter turnout among young people to their lack of connection with their communities, their mistrust of government, and the lack of information available to them regarding candidates and issues.

As you read, consider the following questions:
1. How does the University of California, Los Angeles's 1997 survey cited by the alliance characterize the political desires and habits of college freshmen?
2. In the Medill School of Journalism's view, what is one reason that nonvoters under the age of thirty feel apathetic toward politics?
3. According to the author, what classroom efforts have been used in an attempt to increase voter turnout among youths?

They say that good habits formed early last a lifetime. Unfortunately, voting is not a habit of many young people, which may be one explanation as to why voter turnout is dismally low in this country. While a pitiful 49 percent of eligible voters showed up at the polls in 1996, an even smaller number of young people voted: According to the U.S. Census, only 32 percent of eligible eighteen to twenty-four year olds exercised their right to vote. If the tide is going to turn on voting practices in this country, more will have to be done to ensure that voting becomes a healthy habit. [In the 2000 elections, voter turnout for eighteen to twenty-four year olds was 32 percent.]

Why Don't Young People Vote?

The University of California, Los Angeles's annual nation-wide survey of college freshmen found that the freshmen surveyed in 1997 had the lowest levels of political interest in the history of the survey. Only 26.7 percent reported that "keeping up to date with political affairs" is an important life goal. Freshmen also have less desire to "influence the polit-ical structure" and are less likely to talk about politics than students in prior surveys.

This extreme apathy is likely to have many causes. A 1996 survey by the Medill School of Journalism found that non-voters under 30 often do not feel connected to their commu-nities, in part because they move often. Young non-voters also tend not to like government institutions. The political turbulence of the 1960's and 70's as well as the call for smaller government during the 1980's and 1990's has, ac-cording to some studies, made a lasting impression on America's youth. Young people aren't convinced that politics makes a difference in their lives.

Another factor contributing to the low voter turnout among young people may be the lack of information about the candidates that satisfies their specific needs and interests. A Media Studies Center survey on the 1996 presidential election found that by April of 1996, half of all voters 60 and over felt they had enough information to decide how to vote. By comparison, five of six voters under age 30 reported that they still needed more information to make up their minds.

Ceasing Civics Education

The public school system has virtually ceased to engage in the kind of civics education that many older members of the discipline remember. Responding to alarming reports about students' ignorance of mathematics, geography, history, and the natural sciences, state legislatures have insisted that the schools increase pupils' exposure to these subjects. No such alarm bells have led to more teaching of civics or government topics. Even when students are taught "social studies," the teachers are not likely to have majored in political science, and the course material is often aimed at increasing students' sense of self-esteem rather than broadening their knowledge of American government and politics. Critics of today's school system allege that young people after their social studies education are far more likely to know about Inca rituals than about the U.S. Constitution. It is likely that if students are not taught American politics at an early age, they don't know enough to balance the media's negative images. I am convinced this is one reason for the alarming declines in enrollment and majors that political science departments all over the country are experiencing. One reason for the American Political Science Association's recent report that job listings declined 14% in 1996 is that college administrators, seeing declining enrollments in political science courses, are either eliminating positions that come open or giving new lines to other departments.

Stephen E. Bennett, *PS: Political Science & Politics*, March 1997.

Efforts to encourage young people to vote range from celebrity appearance on MTV to mock elections in schools across the country. Rock the Vote, an organization that in 1996 aimed at increasing voter registration among young people, intends to expand its outreach and education efforts to include civic involvement as well as voter registration. Its "Rock the Nation" program will sponsor public service announcements featuring young people who are making a difference in their communities. Related "Rock the City" forums will bring young people together with community organizations to discuss local issues. In addition, Rock the Vote will produce a community action guidebook—to be distributed in record stores nationwide—designed to show young adults how to access the political system. Rock the Vote has also teamed up with MCI and AARP Research

Center to create NetVote '98, a web site that allows individuals to register to vote on the Internet. Finally, in an attempt to make young people more aware of issues, Rock the Vote's Rock the System has created a web site that covers timely issues from a youth perspective. For instance, a report about health care focuses on sexually transmitted diseases, AIDS and teen pregnancy.

Grassroots efforts to improve youth voter turnout cropped up in 1996 and will continue. Kids Voting USA, for example, tries to combat low turnout by allowing students to join their parents casting ballots on Election Day at official polling sites. Prior to Election Day, the group sponsors classroom activities to teach young people "the importance of being informed and the responsibilities of voting."

Another effort to increase voter turnout by engaging students in the classroom is the National Student/Parent Mock Election program. It conducts voter education activities that culminate in a simulated nationwide election. Project Vote Smart's Vote Smart Classroom likewise uses lesson plans to educate students about the voting process and how to evaluate candidates and elected officials. Lessons include "Who Represents ME?" and "How Congress Works." Project Vote Smart provides both election and off year activities and suggestions for teachers.

The area that could perhaps have the most impact on getting young people involved—the mainstream media—may also be the least involved in targeting political coverage to a younger audience. In 1996, CNN invited a number of under-30 correspondents to report on issues that concerned "Generation X." However, even one of their young commentators, Farai Chideya, told *The Weekly Standard* that the typical news story fails to engage young people, noting: "If it's an education piece, teachers are interviewed, administrators are interviewed. Students have to be interviewed too." Unfortunately, there is little evidence that other broadcasters are paying attention to Chideya's advice, nor are they following CNN's lead. The media's failure to make young people aware of issues is perhaps the biggest obstacle to increasing voter turnout among that age group, and may undermine other youth voter registration efforts.

> "*Young people possess many qualities which can strengthen any department, staff or crew.*"

Most Young People Possess Positive Work Values

Robert D. Ramsey

Employers are often cautious when hiring today's teenagers because they are thought to lack positive work ethics. In the following viewpoint, Robert D. Ramsey claims that the common perceptions of teenagers—that they are lazy, unskilled, materialistic, and delinquent—are myths. Instead, he claims that teens have unique traits that can enhance any workforce, such as enthusiasm, street smarts, and computer skills. Ramsey is an author and expert in supervision and personnel management.

As you read, consider the following questions:

1. According to Ramsey, what has shaped adults' negative views of young people?
2. In the author's view, how are teenagers doing in school?
3. List three characteristics that Ramsey claims teenagers bring to the workforce.

Excerpted from "Should You Hire Today's Teenagers?" by Robert D. Ramsey, *Supervision*, January 2001. Copyright © 2001 by National Research Bureau. Reprinted with permission.

Unprepared. Unruly. Unmotivated. This is how many adults, including some top business leaders, describe today's teenagers. Every society bad mouths its youth; but teen-bashing seems to have reached a peak in America.

We've all read the headlines about school shootings, gang violence, juvenile crime, drug use and teen pregnancies. We've all heard about the dumbing down of our schools. We've all seen the spiked hair, tattoos and pierced body parts. It's no wonder many supervisors and managers are hesitant to employ young people—even when workers are scarce. You may be one of them.

But are you missing a bet? Should you hire today's teenagers? Is the prevailing negative perception of teens fact or fiction? Many educators say it's a myth.

Four Myths About Teenage Workers

Of course, some young people are bad risks as employees. But so are some adults. The professionals who work most closely with today's youth believe our future is in good hands. They say today's teenagers are a lot smarter, stronger, braver and more capable than they get credit for.

If your factory, shop or office needs good help at reasonable wages, maybe it's time to debunk the conventional wisdom about hiring the younger generation. According to many teachers and administrators, here's what's true and what's not about this generation of teenage workers:

Myth #1. Kids today lack fundamental knowledge and basic skills.

There's something wrong with this picture. Actually, college entrance exam scores are on the rise. All across the country, more students are meeting state-mandated graduation standards than ever before. Likewise, the rankings of U.S. students compared to those of other nations are improving.

Most educators also agree any random sample of adults chosen off the street would be hard-pressed to beat a group of randomly selected students from any typical high school in a general knowledge challenge competition.

Even more important than test scores or general knowledge, today's students have greater computer skills than any previous generation. They easily have greater technological know-how than their parents (and most potential employers). After all, who programs your VCR?

Myth #2. Kids today are drug-crazed juvenile delinquents.

Surprise. Most teenagers don't belong to gangs. Most don't even carry guns. Better yet, reports of youth crime and adolescent drug use are down in most major cities across the country.

Even tobacco use has plummeted among today's older teens. Many student leaders are now helping to develop a nationwide educational campaign to counteract exploitive advertising by the tobacco industry.

The Most Ambitious Generation

Large numbers of [young people today] expect to become physicians, lawyers, and business managers; few want to work as machinists, secretaries, or plumbers. Such high ambitions are held by teenagers from all families—rich, poor, Asian, black, Hispanic, and white. More adolescents than ever expect to graduate from college, earn graduate degrees, and work in the white-collar world of professionals. They are America's most ambitious teenage generation ever.

Barbara Schneider and David Stevenson, *The Ambitious Generation: America's Teenagers, Motivated but Directionless*, 1999.

Today's generation of teenagers probably smokes, drinks and does drugs too much. So did yours. The bottom line, according to many educators, is current teenagers aren't as bad as you've been led to believe. Best of all, research shows teens who succeed on the job exhibit fewer at-risk behaviors off the job.

Myth #3. Kids today are lazy, spoiled and have no work ethic.

The truth is this is probably the busiest generation of teenagers ever. Some teens, like some grown-ups, are shiftless and unmotivated; but many young people today carry a full course load at school, keep up with their homework, participate in sports and other activities, volunteer in their communities, find time for a social life and work part-time as well. Some even hold down two or three jobs while keeping up with the rest of their commitments.

That's not lazy. That's a miracle!

Myth #4. Kids today are self-absorbed, materialistic and uncaring.

This is another false perception according to many parents and teachers. Like all generations of young people, today's teens are idealistic, optimistic and altruistic. They want to help others and build a better world just as much as preceding generations.

The class of 2000 is volunteering at record levels. As an example, more and more schools are introducing community service opportunities into the curriculum and students are signing up in large numbers.

That's why it's no accident a growing number of communities have initiated Caring Youth Recognition Programs to honor young people whose volunteer contributions serve as a model for peers and adults alike.

Despite all the myths, then, if we are to believe those who know kids best, hiring this generation of teenage workers may be too good a deal for supervisors to pass up.

What Today's Teenagers Bring to the Workplace

When you hire teenagers, you're not buying maturity or experience; but young people possess many qualities which can strengthen any department, staff or crew.

The most important traits which teens bring to the workforce are the four E's:

1. Energy
2. Enthusiasm
3. Excitement
4. Eagerness to prove themselves

If your workforce is in a rut, the infusion of a few teens can breathe new life into the organization. Teens are anything but boring.

Other important characteristics which young people can add to your employee mix include:

- unflagging optimism
- street smarts
- stamina, quick reflexes and resiliency
- fast track learning ability
- willingness to try almost anything
- total comfort with technology
- youthful creativity and flexibility
- enough innocence and naiveté to challenge the status quo

If these are attitudes and skills you are looking for in

new employees, it's time to rethink any reluctance to hire today's teenagers.

Champion Performers for the Future

The best workforce is a balanced workforce. A variety of competencies, talents, viewpoints and life experiences make a more lively and resourceful staff or crew. Young people are often a welcome addition. The trick is to recruit and hire only the best teenage workers available. . . .

When unemployment is at a record low, it's a mistake for supervisors to ignore a huge pool of potential workers just because they are still minors.

When you hire teenagers, you may be doing more than just filling in some unwanted gaps in your workforce for now. You may also be lining up your champion performers for the future.

| *"Most [young people] have not yet developed
| positive work values."*

Most Young People Do Not Possess Positive Work Values

David J. Cherrington and J. Owen Cherrington

David J. Cherrington and J. Owen Cherrington are co-founders of Cherrington Hayes Cherrington (CHC) Fore-cast, a company that aims to help organizations improve their productivity and profitability. In the following view-point, Cherrington and Cherrington assert that today's youth do not enter the workforce as motivated workers. The authors maintain that today's adolescents have lived in such prosperous and peaceful times compared with youths of the past that they do not know the value of hard work and sacri-fice. In consequence, employers must help them to develop positive work values.

As you read, consider the following questions:
1. According to Cherrington and Cherrington, what rights and privileges are eighteen-year-olds entitled to?
2. In the authors' view, how has television affected young people?
3. List three suggestions Cherrington and Cherrington make to assist young workers in developing positive work values.

From "Preparing for the Next Generation," by David J. Cherrington and J. Owen Cherrington, www.chcforecast.com, 1998. Copyright © 1998 by Cherrington Hayes Cherrington Forecast, Inc. Reprinted with permission.

Every generation of adults faces the daunting responsibility of helping the next generation of youth become mature responsible adults, a process called *socialization*. The job of socialization involves teaching young people the attitudes and values that are considered socially acceptable and making certain their behaviors are consistent with our cultural norms.

The greatest responsibility for socializing children belongs to parents, and there is little doubt that family influences have by far the greatest impact on the social values of children. But the influence of parents can only go so far—children need to hear other voices in society. Education has always played an important role in teaching social values, but the effectiveness of school systems has been reduced by uncertainty about which values should be taught and how they should be presented.

Employers also need to play an important role. If employers want dedicated, honest, moral, and diligent workers, they may have to assume a significant part of the socialization burden and help young workers become mature, responsible adults.

Very Different Perspectives

In 1998, over four million teenagers turned eighteen—the age when society accepts them as mature, responsible adults. They are old enough to vote, old enough to have a driver's license, and old enough to borrow money and sign contracts without their parent's approval. Most of them have entered the labor force, at least part-time, and the vast majority work in the service and retail industries. Most of them handle sizable sums of money for their employers and some hold important positions of responsibility.

Although all of them should have graduated from high school, only about 82 percent of them achieved this noble goal. About half of the drop-outs will eventually obtain a high school diploma through some form of alternative education; but the other half will go through life without a high school education.

The people who turned eighteen in 1998 were born in 1980. Consequently, they will likely have very different perspectives on many of the political, social, and economic issues than older people. Politically, they don't remember much of the President Ronald Reagan era and most of them don't know he was ever shot. They were only eleven when the Soviet Union disintegrated, and they have only known one Germany. Consequently, they have no memory of the Cold War and the real threat it presented of a nuclear war. To them "The Day After" is a pill, not a movie.

They have never lived through a major world war. They weren't around when graphic images of the Vietnam War were flashed across television screens in living color; the Vietnam War is as distant to them as World War I, World War II, or even the Civil War. Even the Persian Gulf War is not a vivid memory to them since it was waged during their prepubescent years. Most of them have no idea that Americans were held hostage in Iran, they do not know who [Libyan leader] Moamar Qadafi is, and Tiananmen Square [center of a 1989 pro-democracy protest in China] means nothing to them.

Most eighteen-year-olds have little or no incentive to save for the future or worry about hard times. They have never heard of "penny postcards." As far as they know, stamps have always cost about 32 cents. Since the economy recovered so quickly from [the stock market crash of] Black Monday in 1987 and the Market Readjustment of 1998, many of them think the Great Depression was "no big thing." To them, WPA[1] and CCCP[2] are just a bunch of letters.

Sony introduced the Walkman the year they were born, and the compact disk emerged when they were one year old. Consequently, the expression, "You sound like a broken record," means nothing to them since most of them have never owned or operated a record player. For the most part, they have never seen a black and white TV or one with only 13 channels; but they have always had an answering machine, a VCR, cable TV, and a remote control. Furthermore, they also assume they should be able to contact anyone, anywhere, at any time.

Most eighteen-year-olds are not prepared to perform

1. The Works Progress Administration was assembled to assist unemployed Americans during the Great Depression.   2. Cyrillic version of USSR, the Union of Soviet Socialist Republics.

repetitive or difficult labor. They think shoes and clothes are made entirely by machines without human effort. They also believe all food is harvested by large combines and other picking machines and the only food picked by hand comes from small gardens that people raise for a hobby. Indeed, many think that all repetitive work has been automated out of existence and robots are used extensively in manufacturing; thus, the primary work of most factory workers is tending and repairing the robots.

Accepting the Media's Message

Unless employers provide effective training and strictly enforce their zero-tolerance policies, they can expect expensive sexual harassment litigation. On average, today's eighteen-year-olds have listened to four hours of music and watched four hours of television per day. Consequently, they think they know what social life is like outside their neighborhood and they have something in common with everyone. Unfortunately, watching TV doesn't develop social skills as well as interacting with friends. So youth who have devoured a heavy diet of television tend to be shy and uncomfortable in social situations. Even more unfortunate, however, is their biased perception of male-female relationships. Since eighty percent of the humor in today's sitcoms is based on sexual innuendos, they have been conditioned to think that all male-female interactions contain sexual undertones of flirtation and seduction. To the extent they have accepted the media's message, they believe all comments between a man and a woman are made against a backdrop of sexual exploration rather than a simple conversation between two adults who have unique personalities and interests that are devoid of sexual fantasy.

Many eighteen-year-olds have never learned respect for authority, because authority figures were absent or ineffective. Accommodating the demands of two-income families often compromises the exposure of children to legitimate authority. Parents who come home exhausted from work are not as likely to involve themselves in working with their children or structuring their lives. Day care providers may be very loving, but they don't have the same power or authority as parents. Two-parent families have twice as many authority figures as single-parent families; and when they are united, the influence of a mother and father is usually perceived as many times more powerful than when either one is acting alone. Other authority figures can be ignored—if students don't like school, they don't have to go; if they don't like their coach, they can quit the team. They never knew the draft, and they haven't been through boot camp.

New Lows

Eighteen-year-olds have witnessed new lows in public displays of integrity and fidelity. The escapades of Hollywood stars have fed the tabloid industry for many years. But more recent sex scandals have plagued some of the most prominent public figures, including the President of the United States, congressional representatives, TV evangelists, the British Monarchy, and professional athletes. The initial responses of these role models were to "lie and deny" until convincing evidence forced them to admit their errors, at which time they tried to assert that it didn't really matter.

The majority of eighteen-year-olds enter the labor force with little or no prior work experience. Although some have learned how to be responsible workers because they worked on farms or other part-time jobs, most have not yet developed positive work values. If employers want these young workers to feel a moral obligation to work diligently and to take pride in their work, they will have to instill these values on the job.

Training the Next Generation

Although most supervisors feel overwhelmed by the challenge of helping young workers acquire positive work values and attitudes, there is much they can do to influence their behavior. The principles for developing positive work values are the principles of good supervision:

1. Establish an organizational climate that fosters positive work values and a commitment to excellence.
2. Communicate clear expectations about productivity and high-quality craftsmanship.
3. Teach and explain the value of work, the dignity of labor, and the joy of service.

4. Establish individual accountability by effectively delegating task assignments.
5. Develop personal commitment and involvement through individual choice and participation.
6. Provide feedback on performance through effective performance appraisals.
7. Reward effective performance with pay and other social reinforcers.
8. Continually encourage employees to improve their skills and further their personal growth and development.

The secret is to be patient and persistent. Supervisors need to set clear quality standards and provide constant feedback on their performance. They also need to be fearless in discussing standards of right and wrong and encouraging them to act ethically. Even teenagers who have learned to be responsible benefit from careful instructions that help them face new challenges. For example, bribes and conflicts of interest are ethical dilemmas they have never faced in their homes and they may need help recognizing them and knowing how to respond to them. Every generation of supervisors faces the challenge of training the next generation.

Periodical Bibliography

The following articles have been selected to supplement the diverse views presented in this chapter.

Kathleen Chesto   "This Is NOT Your Father's Religion," *U.S. Catholic*, July 2001.

Curriculum Administrator   "Study: Widespread Lying and Cheating Among Nation's Teens," December 2000.

Beth Frerking   "A Truer Picture of Teens' Lives," *American Journalism Review*, November 2000.

Susan Gembroski   "Life Goes On in a Troubled World," *San Diego Union-Tribune*, November 11, 2001.

David Holstrom   "Young People Seek Meaning in a Material World," *Christian Science Monitor*, August 7, 1998.

Lisa Miller   "Rebels with a Cause," *Wall Street Journal*, December 18, 1998.

Kim Peterson   "Living in a Material World," *San Diego Union-Tribune*, September 9, 2001.

Peter Ruehl   "Smells Like Teen Spirit," *Business Review Weekly*, March 23, 2001.

Michael Ryan and Lee Kravitz   "Together We Transform the World," *Parade*, September 5, 1999.

David Shaw   "Kids Are People Too, Papers Decide," *Los Angeles Times*, July 11, 2000.

Mark Strama   "Overcoming Cynicism: Youth Participation and Electoral Politics," *National Civic Review*, Spring 1998.

Stacy A. Teicher   "If Any Kid Could Be President, Few Want the Job," *Christian Science Monitor*, March 2, 1999.

Daniel R. Weinberger   "A Brain Too Young for Good Judgment," *New York Times*, March 10, 2001.

CHAPTER 4

How Can Society Help America's Youth?

Chapter Preface

To help at-risk youths get their lives on the right track, the U.S. Department of Labor established Job Corps, a residential program aimed at improving disadvantaged youths' lives through academic, vocational, and life-skills training. Job Corps is open to eligible youths aged sixteen to twenty-four. Participants typically live full time at Job Corps centers, where they are held to strict behavioral standards. At the centers, youths attend academic and vocational classes from six months to two years, depending on the training they receive.

Advocates of Job Corps claim that the program has a lasting, beneficial impact on its graduates. According to National Job Corps chair LaVera Leonard, "Nationally 70 percent of all Job Corps students get jobs or pursue further education." In addition, 85 percent of students receive "impressive reading and math gains." Also, Job Corps maintains that since it was founded in 1964, it has helped 1.9 million youths achieve independence, either by enhancing their career opportunities or helping them achieve their educational goals.

However, detractors argue that the long-term benefits of Job Corps training are overestimated. Sean Paige, editorial director at the Competitive Enterprise Institute, argues that although the U.S. Department of Labor "in 1996 reported that 62 percent of Job Corps participants were putting their skills to work in the private sector, a closer look at the statistics casts doubt on 41 percent of those purported job placements. Oftentimes, kids trained in masonry or health care were instead found flipping burgers or waiting tables—jobs acquired easily enough without a $15,000 taxpayer investment." In addition, a study by the U.S. General Accounting Office claims that two-thirds of Job Corps graduates "did not find employment or found a low-paying job that did not use the skills they had learned."

It is important to debate the effectiveness of widely implemented youth programs such as Job Corps so that young people are given the best chances to succeed. In the following chapter, the authors suggest what they believe are the best ways that society can help America's youth meet the challenges of today and the future.

"The decline of fatherhood is a major force behind many of the most disturbing problems that plague American society."

Society Must Help Fathers Stay Involved in Youths' Lives

David Popenoe

In the following viewpoint, David Popenoe claims that society can help youths by supporting the father's role in the family. Popenoe insists that fathering aids children's behavioral and intellectual development in ways that mothering cannot. According to the author, the prevalence of fatherlessness has exacerbated the problems of youth drug abuse, delinquency, violence, and pregnancy. Popenoe is a sociology professor and author of *Disturbing the Nest: Family Change and Decline in Modern Society*.

As you read, consider the following questions:

1. What is the current cultural view of fatherhood, as stated by Popenoe?
2. How does Popenoe support his assertion that men are not biologically attuned to being committed to fatherhood?
3. In addition to fatherlessness, what other factors does the author cite as threats to children's well-being?

Excerpted from "A World Without Fathers: Consequences of Children Living Without Fathers," by David Popenoe, *Wilson Quarterly*, March 1, 1996. Copyright © 1996 by David Popenoe. Reprinted by permission of Simon and Schuster, Inc.

The decline of fatherhood is one of the most basic, unexpected, and extraordinary social trends of our time. Its dimensions can be captured in a single statistic: in just three decades, between 1960 and 1990, the percentage of children living apart from their biological fathers more than doubled, from 17 percent to 36 percent. By the turn of the century, nearly 50 percent of American children may be going to sleep each evening without being able to say good night to their dads.

No one predicted this trend, few researchers or government agencies have monitored it, and it is not widely discussed, even today. But the decline of fatherhood is a major force behind many of the most disturbing problems that plague American society: crime and delinquency; premature sexuality and out-of-wedlock births to teenagers; deteriorating educational achievement; depression, substance abuse, and alienation among adolescents; and the growing number of women and children in poverty.

The current generation of children and youth may be the first in our nation's history to be less well off—psychologically, socially, economically, and morally—than their parents were at the same age. The United States, observes Senator Daniel Patrick Moynihan (D.-N.Y.), "may be the first society in history in which children are distinctly worse off than adults."

Even as this calamity unfolds, our cultural view of fatherhood itself is changing. Few people doubt the fundamental importance of mothers. But fathers? More and more, the question of whether fathers are really necessary is being raised. Many would answer no, or maybe not. And to the degree that fathers are still thought necessary, fatherhood is said by many to be merely a social role that others can play: mothers, partners, stepfathers, uncles and aunts, grandparents. Perhaps the script can even be rewritten and the role changed—or dropped. . . .

A Monumental Setback

Not so long ago, the change in the cause of fatherlessness was dismissed as irrelevant in many quarters, including among social scientists. Children, it was said, are merely losing their parents in a different way than they used to. You don't hear that very much anymore. A surprising finding of recent social science research is that it is decidedly worse for a child to lose a father in the modern, voluntary way than through death. The children of divorced and never-married mothers are less successful in life by almost every measure than the children of widowed mothers. The replacement of death by divorce as the prime cause of fatherlessness, then, is a monumental setback in the history of childhood. . . .

In theory, divorce need not mean disconnection. In reality, it often does. One large survey in the late 1980s found that about one in five divorced fathers had not seen his children in the past year, and less than half of divorced fathers saw their children more than several times a year. A 1981 survey of adolescents who were living apart from their fathers found that 52 percent had not seen them at all in more than a year; only 16 percent saw their fathers as often as once a week. Moreover, the survey showed fathers' contact with their children dropping off sharply with the passage of time after the marital breakup.

The picture grows worse. Just as divorce has overtaken death as the leading cause of fatherlessness, out-of-wedlock births are expected to surpass divorce later in the 1990s. They accounted for 30 percent of all births by 1991; by the turn of the century they may account for 40 percent of the total (and 80 percent of minority births). And there is substantial evidence that having an unmarried father is even worse for a child than having a divorced father.

Across time and cultures, fathers have always been considered essential—and not just for their sperm. Indeed, until today, no known society ever thought of fathers as potentially unnecessary. Marriage and the nuclear family— mother, father, and children—are the most universal social institutions in existence. In no society has the birth of children out of wedlock been the cultural norm. To the contrary, a concern for the legitimacy of children is nearly universal.

Problematic for Men

At the same time, being a father is universally problematic for men. While mothers the world over bear and nurture their young with an intrinsic acknowledgment and, most commonly, acceptance of their role, the process of taking on the role of father is often filled with conflict and doubt. The source of this sex-role difference can be plainly stated. Men are not biologically as attuned to being committed fathers as women are to being committed mothers. The evolutionary logic is clear. Women, who can bear only a limited number of children, have a great incentive to invest their energy in rearing children, while men, who can father many offspring, do not. Left culturally unregulated, men's sexual behavior can be promiscuous, their paternity casual, their commitment to families weak. This is not to say that the role of father is foreign to male nature. Far from it. Evolutionary scientists tell us that the development of the fathering capacity and high paternal investments in offspring—features not common among our primate relatives—have been sources of enormous evolutionary advantage for human beings.

Ramirez. © 1993 by Copley News Service. Reprinted with permission.

In recognition of the fatherhood problem, human cultures have used sanctions to bind men to their children, and of course the institution of marriage has been culture's chief vehicle. Marriage is society's way of signaling that the community approves and encourages sexual intercourse and the birth of children, and that the long-term relationship of the parents is socially important. Margaret Mead once said, with the fatherhood problem very much in mind, that there is no society in the world where men will stay married for very long unless culturally required to do so. Our experience in late-20th-century America shows how right she was. The results for children have been devastating.

In my many years as a sociologist, I have found few other bodies of evidence that lean so much in one direction as this one: on the whole, two parents—a father and a mother—are better for a child than one parent. There are, to be sure, many factors that complicate this simple proposition. We all know of a two-parent family that is truly dysfunctional—the proverbial family from hell. A child can certainly be raised to a fulfilling adulthood by one loving parent who is wholly devoted to the child's well-being. But such exceptions do not invalidate the rule any more than the fact that some three-pack-a-day smokers live to a ripe old age casts doubt on the dangers of cigarettes.

Consequences of Fatherlessness

The collapse of children's well-being in the United States has reached breathtaking proportions. Juvenile violent crime has increased sixfold, from 16,000 arrests in 1960 to 96,000 in 1992, a period in which the total number of young people in the population remained relatively stable. Reports of child neglect and abuse have quintupled since 1976, when data were first collected. Eating disorders and rates of depression have soared among adolescent girls. Teen suicide has tripled. Alcohol and drug abuse among teenagers, although it has leveled off in recent years, continues at a very high rate. Scholastic Aptitude Test scores have declined nearly 80 points, and most of the decline cannot be accounted for by the increased academic diversity of students taking the test. Poverty has shifted from the elderly to the young. Of all the nation's poor today, 38 percent are children.

One can think of many explanations for these unhappy developments: the growth of commercialism and consumerism, the influence of television and the mass media, the decline of religion, the widespread availability of guns and addictive drugs, and the decay of social order and neighborhood relationships. None of these causes should be dismissed. But the evidence is now strong that the absence of fathers from the lives of children is one of the most important causes.

The most tangible and immediate consequence of fatherlessness for children is the loss of economic resources. By the best recent estimates, the income of the household in which a child remains after a divorce instantly declines by about 21 percent per capita on average, while expenses tend to go up. Over time, the economic situation for the child often deteriorates further. The mother usually earns considerably less than the father, and children cannot rely on their fathers to pay much in the way of child support. About half of previously married mothers receive no child support, and for those who do receive it, both the reliability and the amount of the payment drop over time.

Child poverty, once endemic in America, reached a historic low point of 14 percent in 1969 and remained relatively stable through the 1970s. Since then, it has been inching back up. Today more than 20 percent of the nation's children (and 25 percent of infants and toddlers) are growing up in poverty.

The loss of fathers' income is the most important cause of this alarming change. By one estimate, 51 percent of the increase in child poverty observed during the 1980s (65 percent for blacks) can be attributed to changes in family structure. Indeed, much of the income differential between whites and blacks today, perhaps as much as two-thirds, can be attributed to the differences in family structure. Not for nothing is it said that marriage is the best antipoverty program of all.

A National Economic Emergency

The proliferation of mother-headed families now constitutes something of a national economic emergency. About a quarter of all family groups with children—more than half of all black family groups—are headed by mothers, which is almost double the 11.5 percent figure in 1970. No other group is so poor, and none stays poor longer. Poverty afflicts nearly one out of every two of these families, but fewer than one in 10 married-couple families. Mother-headed families account for 94 percent of the current caseload for Aid to Families with Dependent Children (AFDC).

Things are likely to get worse before they get better. Poverty is much more severe among unmarried mothers— the fastest-growing segment of the poverty population— than among divorced mothers.

Economic difficulties—which translate into poorer schooling and other handicaps—ultimately account for a considerable share of the disadvantages found among fatherless children. By the best recent estimates, however, economic status accounts for no more than half of these disadvantages. The latest and most authoritative review of this research is *Growing Up with a Single Parent*, by sociologists Sara McLanahan of Princeton University and Gary Sandefur of the University of Wisconsin. Reviewing five large-scale social surveys and other evidence (and after adjusting for many income-related factors), they concluded: "Children who grow up with only one of their biological parents (nearly always the mother) . . . are twice as likely to drop out of high school, 2.5 times as likely to become teen mothers, and 1.4 times as likely to be idle—out of school and out of work—as children who grow up with both parents.". . .

What Do Fathers Do?

What do fathers do? Much of what they contribute to the growth of their children, of course, is simply the result of being a second adult in the home. Bringing up children is demanding, stressful, and often exhausting. Two adults can not only support and spell each other; they can offset each other's deficiencies and build on each other's strengths.

Beyond being merely a second adult or third party, fathers —men bring an array of unique and irreplaceable qualities that women do not ordinarily bring. Some of these are familiar, if sometimes overlooked or taken for granted. The father as protector, for example, has by no means outlived his usefulness. His importance as a role model has become a familiar idea. Teenage boys without fathers are notoriously prone to trouble. The pathway to adulthood for daughters is somewhat easier, but they still must learn from their fathers, as they cannot from their mothers, how to relate to men. They learn from their fathers about heterosexual trust, intimacy, and difference. They learn to appreciate their own femininity from the one male who is most special in their lives (assuming that they love and respect their fathers). Most important, through loving and being loved by their fathers, they learn that they are love-worthy.

Recent research has given us much deeper—and more surprising insights into the father's role in child rearing. It shows that in almost all of their interactions with children, fathers do things a little differently from mothers. What fathers do—their special parenting style—is not only highly complementary to what mothers do but is by all indications important in its own right for optimum child rearing.

For example, an often-overlooked dimension of fathering is play. From their children's birth through adolescence, fathers tend to emphasize play more than caretaking. This may be troubling to egalitarian feminists, and it would indeed be wise for most fathers to spend more time in caretaking. Yet the father's style of play seems to have unusual significance. It is likely to be both physically stimulating and exciting. With older children it involves more physical games and teamwork requiring the competitive testing of physical and mental skills. It frequently resembles an apprenticeship or teaching relationship: come on, let me show you how.

Mothers tend to spend more time playing with their children, but theirs is a different kind of play. Mothers' play tends to take place more at the child's level. Mothers provide the child with the opportunity to direct the play, to be in charge, to proceed at the child's own pace. Kids, at least in the early years, seem to prefer to play with daddy. In one study of 2½-year-olds who were given a choice, more than two thirds chose to play with their father.

A Distinctive Role to Play

The way fathers play has effects on everything from the management of emotions to intelligence and academic achievement. It is particularly important in promoting the essential virtue of self-control. According to one expert, "children who roughhouse with their fathers . . . usually quickly learn that biting, kicking, and other forms of physical violence are not acceptable." They learn when enough is enough and when to "shut it down.". . .

It is ironic, however, that in our public discussion of fathering, it's seldom acknowledged that fathers have a distinctive role to play. Indeed, it's far more often said that fathers should be more like mothers (and that men generally should be more like women—less aggressive, less competitive). While such things may be said with the best of intentions, the effects are perverse. After all, if fathering is no different from mothering, males can easily be replaced in the home by women. It might even seem better to do so. Already viewed as a burden and obstacle to self-fulfillment, fatherhood thus comes to seem superfluous and unnecessary as well.

We know, however, that fathers—and fatherlessness—have surprising impacts on children. Fathers' involvement seems to be linked to improved quantitative and verbal skills, improved problem-solving ability, and higher academic achievement. Several studies have found that the presence of the father is one of the determinants of girls' proficiency in mathematics. And one pioneering study found that the amount of time fathers spent reading was a strong predictor of their daughters' verbal ability.

For sons, who can more directly follow their fathers' example, the results have been even more striking. A number of studies have uncovered a strong relationship between father involvement and the quantitative and mathematical abilities of their sons. Other studies have found a relationship between paternal nurturing and boys' verbal intelligence.

How fathers produce these intellectual benefits is not yet clear. No doubt it is partly a matter of the time and money a man brings to his family. But it is probably also related to the unique mental and behavioral qualities of men; the male sense of play, reasoning, challenge, and problem solving, and the traditional male association with achievement and occupational advancement.

Fathers and "Soft" Virtues

Men also have a vital role to play in promoting cooperation and other "soft" virtues. We don't often think of fathers in connection with the teaching of empathy, but involved fathers, it turns out, may be of special importance for the development of this important character trait, essential to an ordered society of law-abiding, cooperative, and compassionate adults. Examining the results of a 26-year longitudinal study, a trio of researchers reached a "quite astonishing" conclusion: the most important childhood factor of all in developing empathy is paternal involvement in child care. Fathers who spent time alone with their children more than twice a week, giving meals, baths, and other basic care, reared the most compassionate adults.

Again, it is not yet clear why fathers are so important in instilling this quality. Perhaps merely by being with their children they provide a model for compassion. Perhaps it has to do with their style of play or mode of reasoning. Perhaps it is somehow related to the fact that fathers typically are the family's main arbiter with the outside world. Or perhaps it is because mothers who receive help from their mates have more time and energy to cultivate the soft virtues. Whatever the reason, it is hard to think of a more important contribution that fathers can make to their children.

Fatherlessness is directly implicated in many of our most grievous social ills. Of all the negative consequences, juvenile delinquency and violence probably loom largest in the public mind. Reported violent crime has soared 550 percent since 1960, and juveniles have the fastest-growing crime rate. Arrests of juveniles for murder, for example, rose 128 percent between 1983 and 1992.

An Excellent Form of Prevention

Many people intuitively believe that fatherlessness is related to delinquency and violence, and the weight of research evidence supports this belief. Having a father at home is no guarantee that a youngster won't commit a crime, but it appears to be an excellent form of prevention. Sixty percent of America's rapists, 72 percent of its adolescent murderers, and 70 percent of its long-term prison inmates come from fatherless homes. Fathers are important to their sons as role models. They are important for maintaining authority and discipline. And they are important in helping their sons to develop both self-control and feelings of empathy toward others.

Unfortunately, the die for the near future has already been cast. The teenage population is expected to grow in the next decade by as much as 20 percent—even more for minority teenagers—as the children of the baby boomers grow up. Many of these restless youngsters will come of age without fathers. Criminologist James Fox warns of "a tremendous crime wave . . . in the next 10 years" fueled by what he calls "the young and the ruthless." In 1993, for example, there were 3,647 teenage killers; by 2005, Fox expects there will be 6,000.

The twin to the nightmare specter of too many little boys with guns is too many little girls with babies. Fatherlessness is again a major contributing factor.

During the past three decades, there has been a dramatic increase in the percentage of teenagers engaging in sexual activity. In the mid-1950s, only 27 percent of girls had sexual intercourse by age 18; in 1988, 56 percent of such girls—including fully a quarter of 15-year-olds—had become sexually active.

About one million teen pregnancies occur in the United States each year, giving this nation the highest teen pregnancy rate in the industrialized world. Twelve percent of all women aged 15 to 19 (21 percent of those who have had sexual intercourse) become pregnant each year. Fifty percent of these pregnancies end in births, 35 percent end in abortions, and about 14 percent end in miscarriages. Of all children born out of wedlock, most will grow up fatherless in single-parent households. . . .

Restore Marriage and Reinstate Fathers

Just as cultural forms can be discarded, dismantled, and declared obsolete, so can they be reinvented. In order to restore marriage and reinstate fathers in the lives of their children, we are somehow going to have to undo the cultural shift of the last few decades toward radical individualism. We are going to have to re-embrace some cultural propositions or understandings that throughout history have been universally accepted but which today are unpopular, if not rejected outright.

Marriage must be re-established as a strong social institution. The father's role must also be redefined in a way that neglects neither historical models nor the unique attributes of modern societies, the new roles for women, and the special qualities that men bring to child rearing.

Such changes are by no means impossible. Witness the transformations wrought by the civil rights, women's, and environmental movements, and even the campaigns to reduce smoking and drunk driving. What is necessary is for large numbers of adults, and especially our cultural and intellectual leaders, to agree on the importance of change. . . .

Government policies should be designed to favor married, child rearing couples. Some critics argue that the federal government should not involve itself in sensitive moral issues or risk stigmatizing alternative lifestyles. But recognizing such alternatives does not require treating them as equivalent to marriage. The government, moreover, regularly takes moral positions on a whole range of issues, such as the rights of women, income equality, and race relations. A position on the need for children to have two committed parents, a father and a mother, during their formative years is hardly a radical departure.

2

"What is important . . . is the quality of the relationships [youths] have with the people who care for them, rather than the number, sex, or marital status of their caregivers."

The Adverse Effects of Fatherlessness Have Been Exaggerated

Louise B. Silverstein and Carl F. Auerbach

Louise B. Silverstein and Carl F. Auerbach are associate professors at the Farkauf Graduate School of Psychology at the Yeshiva University in New York. In the following viewpoint, Silverstein and Auerbach contend that youths raised in fatherless families are as well adjusted as youths raised in father-headed nuclear families. The authors oppose the assertion that fatherlessness contributes to juvenile crime and teen pregnancy. According to Silverstein and Auerbach, studies claiming to establish the relationship between fatherlessness and troubled youths are actually documenting the negative effects of poverty.

As you read, consider the following questions:

1. As stated by the authors, what is the family values perspective?
2. According to the authors, how does trying to conform to the "myth of the normal family" affect parents heading nontraditional families?
3. How do Silverstein and Auerbach support their argument that boys do not need male role models to become well-adjusted men?

From "The Myth of the 'Normal' Family," by Louise B. Silverstein and Carl F. Auerbach, *USA Today*, January 2001. Copyright © 2001 by the Society for the Advancement of Education. Reprinted with permission.

O ur cultural mythology about parenting is that there is "one right way" to raise children. Most people believe that the best way to raise children is with both a stay-at-home mother (at least while the kids are young) and a bread-winner father in a long-term marriage that lasts "till death do us part." We have been told that any family that is different from this norm shortchanges youngsters.

This point of view has become known as the family values perspective. However, the majority of families do not fit this model. Most mothers have to, or want to, be part of the paid workforce; about half of all marriages will end in divorce; and many more people than ever before will choose to have children without getting married.

New scientific information has emerged in the last 11 years that contradicts the idea that there is one right way. We now know that children can thrive in many different family forms. The scientific evidence shows conclusively that what is important for them is the quality of the relationships they have with the people who care for them, rather than the number, sex, or marital status of their caregivers.

Nevertheless, perfectly normal families that do not fit into the traditional mold feel abnormal and berate themselves for providing their offspring with an inferior version of family life. For these parents, trying to conform to the Myth of the Normal Family often generates guilt, anxiety, power struggles, and other stress.

The Myth of Father Absence

The Myth of Father Absence maintains that most social problems—like juvenile violence, crime, and teen pregnancy—are caused by the lack of a father. If every child had a father, these social problems would disappear, argue the advocates of this viewpoint.

Susan and John, a middle-class African-American couple, had two boys aged six and 10 when Susan came into therapy asking for help to work out her marital problems. John attended one or two sessions, but then refused to come to therapy. John was a devoted father in terms of spending time with the boys. The marital problems were caused because he was often out of work. He had difficulty getting along with bosses and had recently begun to smoke marijuana.

John was a bright man, but always had difficulty in school. He had graduated from high school with a great deal of tutoring and had gone to junior college briefly. From his description of his struggles in school, he probably had an undiagnosed learning disability. Because these problems had not been understood, John had not gotten the help he needed, and he felt stupid. This sense of inadequacy about his intelligence was probably at the root of his difficulty in getting along with superiors and his retreat into drugs.

Susan, in contrast, had always done well in school. She had become a licensed practical nurse and was going to night school to become a registered nurse. She often worked additional hours on the weekends in a nursing home so that the boys could attend parochial school. She was exhausted from this difficult work schedule and the responsibility for all of the cooking and housework. Her stress was exacerbated by the fact that, in the last year, she was frequently the only breadwinner, as John had been fired from several jobs.

Over the next eight years, John's drug problems became much worse. He began using and selling cocaine. When he was using, he often became physically violent with Susan. Although he continued to share responsibility for child care, John was mostly out of work.

The Myth of the Male Role Model

Susan stated that she wanted to leave John, but just could not bring herself to do it. She knew that their fights were frightening to the children and that seeing their father in bad shape was not helpful to them. Still, she could not convince herself to separate from her husband. Despite the fact that she was functioning as both caregiver and breadwinner, she believed that her boys needed their father. She worried that leaving John would mean that she was the stereotypical "black matriarch" who emasculated her man. Most important, she feared that, if John left, the boys would become involved with gangs, drop out of school, and generally get into trouble.

Did it make sense for Susan to stay in a marriage that was not working for her, for John, or for her children? If she did decide to raise the boys on her own, would they really be more likely to get into trouble than if she stayed in a marriage with a husband who was abusing her and cocaine?

The Myth of the Male Role Model is based on the premise that boys have a special need for fathers because only a male role model can teach a boy how to become a man.

Sharon is a physician. She is a very bright, no-nonsense kind of woman who feels more comfortable in the operating room than in a dating situation. She has always liked men and gotten along well with them, but had difficulty establishing and maintaining a romantic relationship. She had one very serious boyfriend in medical school, but they broke up after four years because of his drinking. After that, she had brief affairs with several other doctors throughout internship and residency training, but none of those relationships ever developed. The men she was involved with always ended up marrying nurses or secretaries, never a doctor.

In her late 30s, she began a relationship with an investment banker who recently had been divorced. He was determined never to get married again and certainly never to have children. He and Sharon were very compatible. However, she really wanted children. When she celebrated her 40th birthday, she decided that she would have to contemplate having children without a man or lose the opportunity to have kids altogether. She contacted a sperm bank and became pregnant through artificial insemination. Her boyfriend decided he did not want to remain in the relationship. Sharon had a relatively easy pregnancy and delivery, and with her new baby boy, she embarked on the adventure of single motherhood. Sharon has felt a great deal of anxiety that she will not be able to teach her son how to be a man. Although her son is now four years old and doing fine, she still worries constantly that he may be permanently scarred by not having a father.

Myths About Gay Families

A major component of the myth of the idealized father is that he cannot be gay.

Many of the gay fathers in our research study forced themselves to deny the fact that they were gay because they wanted to be fathers. As one of them put it, "Being gay and being a father seemed mutually exclusive." These men desperately wanted to be "normal" which was defined as being married and having children. They tried to fit themselves into the mold of a married man, hoping against hope that getting married would save them from being gay.

Tom is one of these men. He met Sheri, his wife, in college, and she became a good friend. He admired her and liked her a lot. Tom is very religious, so he prayed that marriage would turn friendship into love. "If Christ could raise the dead, I thought that he could surely cure a homosexual," he reasoned.

More Needed and Valued

Young people may feel more needed and valued as contributing members [in a single-parent] household. I still remember Mom's "duty lists" she gave out each Saturday. All five of us were expected to fulfill our responsibilities. Failure to do so only placed increased burdens on Mom. In two-parent families, parents typically share the major responsibilities. In single-parent families, each child's help is needed and vital in day-to-day living. As a result, they may feel more valued.

Steve Duncan, *Montana State University Communications Series*, December 20, 1995.

Although he and Sheri developed a relationship of mutual respect, they were not in love. Yet, when they had children, they were both so pleased with becoming parents that the kids provided a sort of glue that kept the marriage together. Tom recalled that he felt so happy bonding with his offspring that he was able to avoid the loneliness he felt in his relationship with Sheri.

However, when their second child was six years old, the pleasure of being a father was no longer enough to compensate for an empty marriage. Tom remembered "the moment my life fell apart"—the day he no longer could deny his homosexuality to himself. He then spent several years in torment, feeling torn between his desire to live with his children and his desire to be true to himself. When he finally got enough courage to leave his marriage, he still did not feel brave enough to admit his homosexuality to his wife or his children. He was terrified that he would lose visitation rights with his kids if the court discovered that he was gay.

To his surprise and sorrow, many of his gay friends were not a source of support on this issue. They were interested in living a single gay lifestyle that did not include children. Thus, he could not admit his identity as a gay man to his family, and his gay friends did not support his identity as a father. He expressed his isolation by saying, "I felt I was the only man on the planet who was a father and was gay."

Did Tom have to feel tortured about being a gay father? Can only straight men be good fathers?

In reviewing the scientific research, we found that there is not a single study showing that a male role model is necessary for boys to become well-adjusted men. We now know that both boys and girls use same-sex and opposite-sex role models: parents, grandparents, and other extended family members; teachers; and cultural heroes. In our own research, many of our subjects stated, "My mother taught me how to be a good father."

Effects of Father Absence or Poverty?

In terms of "fatherless" families, it is important to point out that the research has been done primarily with poor, ethnic minority families. Because more single-mother families are poor, it is difficult to differentiate the effects of father absence from the effects of poverty. When we look at the research on middle-class lesbian-mother families, we find that the children being raised in these fatherless families are doing just fine. These youngsters score within the normal range on measures of intelligence, social behavior, and emotional well-being. This finding suggests that the studies focusing on poor, mother-headed families are actually studying the effect of poverty, rather than the absence of a father.

Studies on children being raised by gay fathers have also shown that children raised in these families are growing up healthy. They do not become gay any more frequently than children raised by heterosexual parents.

The people cited above were able to establish a sense of psychological security only after they stopped trying to live up to a family values ideal that simply did not fit their realities. Susan's story is a dramatic example of trying to live up to the cultural mythology about fathers and families, even when it flies in the face of one's better judgment. Susan's decision to stay with John was not helpful to herself, her sons, or John. When she left him, he finally sought help for his drug addiction. He ultimately got and kept a good job, remarried, and became a financially responsible father to his sons and stepdaughter.

Sharon's story is another example of how the family values point of view generates unnecessary stress. Although Sharon worries about raising her son without a father, she is not raising him without a man. In fact, he has close relationships with several men.

Her first cousin is his godfather and spends every Sunday with him. One of his usual babysitters is another cousin of hers, a male student who loves kids and needs spending money. Moreover, Sharon's father comes to stay with her for several weeks three times a year. The presence of men in the life of a single mother is not unusual. Most women have men in their lives.

Finally, Tom is the same father as an openly gay male that he was as a married man. His relationship with his teenage children did not deteriorate when he told them he was gay; rather, their relationship deepened. The kids' immediate reaction was, "Oh, Dad, we've known that for a long time! Tell us something we don't know." Tom reported that he felt so reassured by their acceptance of him that he has since been able to establish a much deeper sense of closeness with them. We are not saying that everything will be easy or will work out fine if only people give up the family values perspective. Instead, we are suggesting that there is no general solution to the complex challenges of family life. Trying to conform to a single version of family life is not just doomed to failure, but unnecessary. Intimate relationships and good-enough parenting are always difficult to achieve. However, if people attempt to conform to idealized myths, they are making the difficult challenge of raising healthy children even more difficult. Rather than trying to find the "one right way," parents need to be flexible and creative in seeking strategies that work for their particular family.

*"Programs are now appearing in schools
and community centers to provide attitudes
and skills to resolve conflict nonviolently."*

Community Programs Can Help Youths

Gene Stephens

Gene Stephens, in the following viewpoint, suggests that
community programs can positively affect the lives of at-risk
youths. For example, Stephens claims that programs that
teach young people the skills to solve conflicts peacefully
ameliorate the problem of youth violence. In addition, he
contends that programs that help build self-esteem through
positive feedback and counseling prevent juvenile delinquency. Stephens is a professor at the College of Criminal
Justice at the University of South Carolina in Columbia.

As you read, consider the following questions:
1. In Stephens's opinion, what factors compound youths'
   social problems?
2. What is positive reinforcement, as described by Stephens?
3. Describe three of the eight suggestions in the author's
   plan for reaching out to troubled youths.

Excerpted from "Youth at Risk: Saving the World's Most Precious Resource," by
Gene Stephens, *The Futurist*, March/April 1997. Copyright © 1997 by World
Future Society. Reprinted with permission.

Growing numbers of children are being neglected, abused, and ignored. Without change, the dark specter of generational warfare could become all too real.

After two decades of study, however, I conclude that we can stop this negative trend and do a better job of nourishing this most important resource. To do otherwise would surely be a violation of our obligation to future generations.

Lost in Society

Child-care advocates claim that up to 15% of 16- to 19-year-olds are at risk of never reaching their potential and simply becoming lost in society. Others would add to this category children of any age if they are at risk of not becoming self-supporting adults, headed for a life in institutions for delinquency, crime, mental illness, addiction, and dependency. We could also describe as "at risk" those teens and preteens who take on child rearing themselves and drop out of school.

The task of saving these children has become increasingly formidable. Compounding the problem are the expanding gap between the rich and poor, the increasing number of single-parent households, the rise of homes where both parents work, the growing gun culture, and the recent increase in negative attitudes about children, such as courts that treat younger and younger children as adult criminals.

As a result, children lose hope for the future. They turn to peers for attention; they turn to guns for protection, security, and status; and they turn to sex and drugs for comfort and relief of boredom. The gang too often becomes their "family"— the only place where they receive attention and approval.

Criminologist James Fox of Northeastern University predicts that the murders committed by teenagers will skyrocket as the 39 million children now under age 10 swell the ranks of teenagers by 20% in the first decade of the twenty-first century. The result could be a juvenile crime wave such as the United States has never seen.

Unrecognized Renaissance

Yet, such a catastrophe is not inevitable. There are some signs of hope: a slightly decreased birth rate among teenagers in the mid-1990s, a rising bipartisan concern about "saving the children," burgeoning community-based experiments for meeting the needs of youth, and a movement to regard poor prenatal care, poor parenting skills, child abuse, and child neglect as public-health problems.

Beyond this, a striking change in the rearing of children in many families has been observed. Countering the trend toward ignoring or even abusing children is a trend toward cherishing and nurturing them. Thousands or even millions of young parents are taking turns working while the other stays at home and makes child care almost a full-time vocation. There is an unrecognized renaissance in parenting progressing quietly in neighborhoods across the nation and possibly the world. . . .

The Best Approaches

Numerous programs have been developed to cope with the at-risk youth population. Here are some of the best approaches.

Positive Reinforcement. Children crave attention more than anything else, especially positive attention. A baby who is cuddled, talked to, and stimulated in the first six weeks of life is much more likely to be intelligent and well adjusted than a baby ignored and simply fed and cleaned up in silence. Later, the child who is rewarded with praise for accomplishments is much more likely than others to become optimistic and achievement oriented.

So how does one extinguish unacceptable behavior? By ignoring it and eliminating the child's ability to gain attention. The simplest examples are having the child sit in a corner or placing the child in a closed room for a short "time out."

For older children, pats on the back, awards, and ceremonies to celebrate accomplishments are particularly effective in fostering prosocial behavior and giving at-risk youth a stake in society, helping them overcome lack of hope and lack of faith in the future. The bottom line: Using positive reinforcement must become a way of life for parents, teachers, and others.

Parent Education. Teaching positive reinforcement to prospective parents has been effective in reducing the at-risk population. Parent education can provide information and skills to assist the parent-to-be with incentives to learn and use good child-rearing practices.

To be effective in reducing teenage parenting, these classes must reach children early—sixth grade or shortly thereafter. In programs that force them to carry a computerized crying and wetting doll around for a couple of weeks, many teenagers decide to postpone parenthood.

Healthy Start. The Justice Department and Health and Human Services each have Healthy Start programs. Justice's program was designed to reduce neglect and abuse, while the Health and Human Services program was designed to reduce infant mortality by strengthening the maternal and infant care systems at the community level.

Ripples of Hope

Not only have AmeriCorps members changed the communities they've worked in for the better—sending ripples of hope across America—they've earned money for college and learned important lessons about themselves in the process. According to Andre Crisp, a 19-year-old, second-year Corps member who spoke at the White House in October 1999: "It's a chance to push yourself past limitations and to do what you never knew you could do."

Controversial when my husband [former President Bill Clinton] first proposed it, AmeriCorps has won the enthusiastic support of leaders across the political spectrum. When asked about AmeriCorps at the National Governors Association conference in September 1999, U.S. Secretary of State Colin Powell said: "It is a tremendous investment in young people, a tremendous investment in the future."

Hillary Clinton, *White House Weekly*, October 25, 1999.

A similar program, Healthy Families America, was launched in 1992 by the National Committee to Prevent Child Abuse to help establish home visitation programs, service networks, and funding opportunities so all new parents can receive the necessary education and support.

Mentoring. To help provide positive adult role models for at-risk youths, leaders in Kansas City are on a quest to recruit, train, and assign 30,000 mentors—one for every at-risk child in the city. Other communities have greatly expanded existing mentoring programs, such as Big Brothers and Big Sisters.

Nonviolent Conflict Resolution. Programs are now appearing in schools and community centers to provide attitudes and skills necessary to resolve conflict nonviolently. Models have been developed by the American Bar Association and the Justice Department, as well as by educators. One of the best models involves training school staff—teachers, administrators, custodians, bus drivers, and cafeteria workers—in creative nonviolent conflict-resolution methods. Older students are also taught these techniques, and they in turn teach younger students, turning peer pressure into a positive rather than negative force.

Community Schools Programs

All communities have schools, but all communities do not use those schools effectively in breaking the cycle of violence and frustration among at-risk youth. A federal initiative—the Community Schools Program—has been effective in rallying the community around the school.

Other examples of successful partnerships include:

- In Missouri, 6,000 volunteers keep 675 schools open for extra hours.
- Boys' and Girls' Clubs offer mentoring in New Jersey schools.
- In New York City, Safe Haven programs provide safe environments and positive after-school tutoring and enrichment programs.
- Year-round schools in many communities facilitate better learning—since students no longer have the long summer to forget what they learned—and foster more opportunities for extracurricular programs, from tutoring and mentoring to family activities and counseling.

Character Education. Character education in schools generally revolves around universally accepted values (e.g., love, truthfulness, fairness, tolerance, responsibility) that find little opposition based on differing political, social, and religious beliefs. Schools with large numbers of at-risk children have reported pregnancy and dropout rates cut in half, along with reduced fights and suspensions, after character education took hold.

Youth Initiatives. Surveys by Gallup Poll, Wirthlin Group, and others consistently find that 95% of teenagers believe it is important for adults and teens "to get involved in local civic, charitable, cultural, environmental, and political activities." More than three-fourths of teens say they are already participating in some volunteer work, such as working at soup kitchens for the poor, nursing homes for the elderly, or shelters for the homeless.

Programs such as AmeriCorps, Job Corps, Peace Corps, and others provide young people a chance to learn the joy of giving to others; at the same time, it gives them a stake in society by developing skills, discipline, and a chance to go to trade school or college through grants and loans. Many communities and even some states (Georgia, for example) are developing youth-oriented community service programs of their own.

Juvenile Justice

Community Policing. Law enforcement programs are increasingly working in partnership with the community to identify crime-breeding problems and implement solutions. Many of the at-risk youths' problems thus become community problems and lend themselves to community solutions. Homelessness, poverty, lack of positive adult role models, and poor health care may lead to safe shelters, community assistance, mentors, and in-school or community clinics.

One of the best examples of this approach took place in Milton Keynes, England, which faced a rash of shoplifting, burglary, and a few store robberies. Rather than seek out, arrest, and prosecute the young offenders, Police Commander Caroline Nicholl instituted a series of conferences in which police, merchants, and neighbors met with offenders and suspects to identify reasons for the offenses. As a result, Nicholl says, "We learned about child abuse, bullying, alcoholism, and many other problems, and the community set to work on these."

Restorative Justice. Most at-risk youth encounter the justice system early in life. Where juvenile justice once focused on the needs of the child, it now focuses on the deeds of the child and a belief that someone, adult or child, has to pay for the offense.

Countering this trend is a restorative justice movement, which holds that the purpose of justice is to bring peace and harmony back to the community by restoring victim, community, and offender to a symbiotic relationship. Often, restoring includes restitution, service, and reclamation.

In the case of juvenile offenders, the child usually makes restitution to the victim either by his or her own earnings or through closely monitored personal service (cutting the lawn, raking leaves, chopping wood, or making home repairs), several hours of service to the community, an apology to the victim, counseling, and essays and/or school talks on the harm the offense does to society. Once the restitution is completed, the child's record is purged.

There are literally hundreds of programs being tried in small and large communities across the nation and, indeed, worldwide.

A Plan

The plan that follows represents a consensus from groups to whom I've given the same assignment over the past decade: "Develop a program to turn your community's youth into productive, happy, law-abiding adults." These groups have included students from high school to graduate school, practitioners from police to social service workers, and community leaders, all participating in brainstorming and planning sessions to alleviate the youth-at-risk problem.

Here is a comprehensive plan based on my 10-plus years' experience with these exercises.

1. Commit to positive reinforcement through community and school-based parenting classes (mandatory in schools), ongoing media campaigns, positive attention, and recognition in all schools (preschool through high school) and community-based programs.

2. Promote nonviolent conflict resolution among peers through mandatory educational programs for students, parents, teachers, counselors, administrators, media, and community campaigns.

3. Encourage mentoring for all children. Civic, business, and community campaigns should recruit and train mentors, matching them by needs and temperament. Programs such

as Big Brothers and Big Sisters should be expanded.

4. Establish community-school partnerships to offer before- and after-school tutoring. Enlist youth to perform services to the community to enhance their stake in society.

5. Develop community-oriented proactive policing programs that begin with a philosophy of prevention. Examples of prevention programs include midnight basketball leagues, police-youth athletic leagues, neighborhood housing project substations, and foot patrols. These all involve partnerships of police, parents, church, business, civic, and community organizations.

6. Initiate ethical and cultural awareness programs that build on partnerships among family, church, school, media, civic, business, and other community groups. These programs would emphasize finding common ground on basic values, such as respect, responsibility, and restraint.

7. Design youth opportunity programs to provide all children the chance to reach their potential, regardless of circumstances. Such programs could be run through school, business, and community partnerships that provide in-school jobs and child care, career counseling and training, opportunity scholarships, and recognition for achievement.

8. Set up peer counseling hotlines to help youth help each other through the trying times of adolescence. . . .

Every community can develop programs guided by this model. But all plans must adopt certain guiding principles that permeate the approach.

Children want attention above everything. Thus, giving attention reinforces behavior and denying attention extinguishes behavior. Both praise and punishment are attention, and both will reinforce behavior that gets that attention.

It is important to instill optimism and faith in the future in all children, as they are the key to success. The very nature of adolescence is to challenge authority, but most children drift through this troubled period and become law-abiding adults unless they become labeled as delinquents, criminals, or losers.

Surely we can see the need to reach out and lend a hand to the world's most precious resource.

*"We are suggesting that [schools] take
seriously their responsibility to awaken and
inspire their students to lead moral lives."*

Schools Should Teach Youths Ethical Values

Kevin Ryan and Karen Bohlin

Many commentators assert that education plays a vital role
in determining the values and moral character of youths. In
the following viewpoint, Kevin Ryan and Karen Bohlin insist that "character education"—in which students are taught
core values in the classroom—is missing from the curriculum of schools nationwide. Among these universally accepted core values are integrity, perseverance, and other
traits that would help young people lead moral lives. Ryan
and Bohlin are authors of *Building Character in Schools: Practical Ways to Bring Moral Instruction to Life.*

As you read, consider the following questions:

1. How do Ryan and Bohlin support their claim that
   educators should teach values in schools?
2. What is one objection to mandating character education
   in school, according to the authors?
3. How do the authors view the status of core values in the
   late 1960s and 1970s?

From "Teacher Education's Empty Suit," by Kevin Ryan and Karen Bohlin,
Education Week, www.edweek.org, March 8, 2000. Copyright © 2000 by Editorial
Projects in Education. Reprinted with permission.

Teaching is intrinsically and unavoidably a moral act. Schools and their classrooms and playgrounds are caldrons of moral matter, ethical issues, and the events that affect a young person's character. Some children slip into the habit of cheating; some become champions of the underdogs; and everyone's image of a good person, a good life, is profoundly affected by their long years in school. But while this may be a masterful grasp of the obvious, few in teacher education are acting upon it.

Teaching Morality

As Greek philosopher Aristotle noted: "We are what we repeatedly do. Excellence, then, is not an act but a habit." Since the time of the Greeks, we have known that teachers, consciously or unconsciously, play a critical role in a child's habit or character formation. In 1984, professor Alan Tom reiterated this fact in his acclaimed book *Teaching as a Moral Act*. In 1990, professor John I. Goodlad, one of America's most influential educators, and his colleagues called the teacher education community to action with their book *The Moral Dimension of Teaching*. Nevertheless, the overwhelming percentage of our teacher-training institutions provide future teachers with neither the preparation nor the mandate they need to help a child toward moral maturity.

In the spring of 1999, the Washington-based Character Education Partnership released a study dealing with what deans and directors of teacher education reported about their institutions' efforts to prepare future teachers as educators of character. Conducted by the Boston University Center for the Advancement of Ethics and Character, the study was based on an eight-page survey that was sent to a random selection of 600 of the 1,400-plus institutions preparing teachers.

Character Education

The respondents were informed that the term "character education" was to be understood in the broadest sense "to encompass the wide range of approaches used by educators to foster good values and character traits in young people." Further, we offered a number of alternative terms that respondents might be more familiar with, terms such as values education, ethics, and moral development. The survey had a respectable 35 percent return rate.

The data from this survey suggest that our current mechanism for preparing future teachers is failing to respond to issues of character formation. Among the major findings are these:

• More than 90 percent of the leadership in teacher education agreed that core values can and should be taught in schools. An even larger number—97 percent—disagreed when the issue was posed in the negative: "Schools should avoid teaching values or influencing moral development. Character education is not the responsibility of the schools."

• There is a large gap between interest or approval and their own programs. Only 13 percent said they were satisfied with their character education efforts. Only 24 percent reported that character education is highly emphasized in their programs. An overwhelming 81 percent said that their efforts to address character education were hindered by the difficulty of "finding room in a crowded curriculum."

• There is little consensus about what character education is and how it should be taught. Schools of education emphasize very different approaches in teaching character education to future teachers, ranging from experiential education to religious education, and from life skills to moral reasoning.

• "Community" is a dominant framework and a powerful metaphor for teacher-educators in their character education efforts. The two most often checked approaches to character education were "caring community" and "service learning." Service learning brings students into direct contact with a larger community through volunteer work, while a caring-community approach focuses on building cooperative, empathetic relationships within the classroom.

• When it comes to character education, most schools of education emphasize applied, hands-on approaches over more directive, academic-centered, and philosophical approaches. The respondents cited the learning process rather than curricular content as the primary vehicle for character education.

• Schools of education with religious ties are more strongly committed to character education than their secular counterparts. The commitment to character education is reflected in many aspects of schools with religious ties, from their mission statements to honor codes, professional oaths, and special rituals and ceremonies. The leadership of several of these schools and departments claimed that "character education is central to their philosophy of education."

• Teacher-educators generally, but cautiously, favor making character education a requirement for state certification. A clear majority—65 percent—support legislation that would require this new regulatory mandate. As one dean put it, "Because values are too important to be left to a hidden curriculum, character education should be a required component of a teacher-certification program." Still, many expressed reservations about overregulating and homogenizing character education through such legislation.

Little Room to Add Something New

The deans and other leaders of teacher education who responded to this study had many reasons for giving no, or very minor, attention in their programs to character education. Prominent among their reasons were the limited time and space in their teacher education curricula. They reported that they were so busy meeting their states' mandated content requirements that they had no opportunity to add new content. In the same vein, they reported that since their accrediting agencies, including the National Council for the Accreditation of Teacher Education and others, placed no emphasis on this topic, they felt they had little leverage to introduce it within their institutions. Other respondents reported being so pressed meeting their states' mandated teacher-education-certification requirements that there was little or no opportunity to add "something new" without the force behind it. Still others cited the continuing struggle within their institutions between general education and professional education that left them little room in a future teacher's program to "add something new."

Besides these related no-room, no-leverage reasons, other factors contribute to the near absence of targeted preparation for the work of character development and the teaching of core ethical values. High among these are the near disappearance of courses in the philosophy of education and the history of education in teacher-preparation programs. Whatever else might be said about the once-required courses, they did engage future teachers with the long tradition of moral education in our schools and in the ethical dimensions of their work with students.

The Institutional Context

Further, there is the institutional context of teacher education. Since the beginning of this century, we have prepared teachers on college and university campuses. Thus, teacher education has not been immune to the intellectual movements and fashions of higher education. In particular, amid the turmoil of the Vietnam War, schools and departments of education distanced themselves from charges that our public schools "indoctrinate" students with the materialistic values of a corrupt capitalistic power structure and America's desire for world hegemony.

Building on Students' Existing Values

The challenge of whose values to teach can be readily addressed by starting with the myriad values we all share. Nobody considers it moral to abuse children, to steal, to commit rape or murder, to be disrespectful to others, to discriminate, and so on. Take the example of date rape. Let's assume that we can all agree that students must realize that using force to impose themselves on others is morally unacceptable. In teaching this value, we run into a "specific," the belief that surprisingly many young males hold that, when a female says "no," she means "yes." Hence it is acceptable to proceed despite her protests. An educator should be able to build on the students' existing value that a "real" no must be heeded and to show that, when a female says no, a decent person restrains himself. If there is any doubt about whether the answer is yes, he should seek further clarification before proceeding. Thus a position on specifics that is morally acceptable to most people can often be worked out when the basic value commitments are in place.

Amitai Etzioni, *Phi Delta Kappan*, February 1998.

In the turbulent social climate of the late 1960s and 1970s, aggressively advocating America's core ethical values on our campuses found few supporters and many energetic critics. And, as many have noted, rather than total abandonment of such a central responsibility of teachers and schools, schools and departments of education embraced a supposedly "value free" approach of helping students come to moral maturity, called "values clarification." Although now widely recognized as an abandonment of the teacher's role, this allegedly non-indoctrinative method still has a strong grip on American education. In the study, only the leadership of programs in private secular (nonreligious) institutions mentioned values clarification as one of the dominant approaches they teach. Still, however, the effects on teachers and teachers-to-be of three decades of dealing with the moral domain of teaching and learning in a relaxed, value-free way linger.

Dulling a Natural Tendency

People enter teaching not simply to dispense information and skills. Many, probably the majority, want to help the young become good people, adults of intelligent substance and character. What they too often receive as preparation, however, are techniques, strategies, and methods, plus a picture of education as riddled with vexing controversies such as creationism, safe sex, and indoctrinative education vs. progressive education. The result of this preparation is to dull their natural tendency to assume their responsibility as adults to pass on our heritage of moral wisdom. Amid all their attention to the supposed "knowledge base for teaching," the importance of shaping character and developing good habits is lost.

Even with what is clearly the growing support from our politicians and the public, restoring the traditional moral authority of teachers and schools will be a long, uphill struggle. The need is great, but it is not going to be easily or quickly remedied. We need more than a mandate—we need a serious examination of the actual content of moral education in teacher-preparation programs.

Awakening Students' Moral Lives

We are not suggesting that teachers learn to force-feed moral principles and precepts to their students. Rather, we are suggesting that they take seriously their responsibility to awaken and inspire their students to lead moral lives. Virtues such as integrity and perseverance find complex and practical expression in history, literature, film, science, and art, and teachers must know how to work these into our academic curricula and the everyday life of the classroom.

Little will be accomplished, however, if the over 2 million new teachers needed in the next 10 years are unprepared to take on their responsibilities as educators of character. As this study demonstrates, the leadership of teacher education (our deans and directors of teacher education) recognize the need, but are either unsure of what to do or unable to put a plan in action. Before any real changes are made, they will need strong help from state departments of education, accrediting agencies, and from within their own institutions. Without this, character education will remain teacher education's empty suit.

> *"Volunteering affords teens both an opportunity to shape their communities and to receive lifelong personal benefits."*

Youths Should Be Encouraged to Volunteer

Independent Sector

Independent Sector is a national coalition of voluntary organizations that promotes volunteering, philanthropy, and citizen action to improve the nation's communities. In the following viewpoint, Independent Sector maintains that youths should get involved in public service in order to reap volunteerism's benefits. Drawing from their 1999 study, *Volunteering and Giving Among Teenagers 12 to 17 Years of Age*, the organization claims that volunteerism engages teens in civic life and gives them opportunities to develop leadership skills.

As you read, consider the following questions:
1. According to Independent Sector, how have religious institutions influenced teens' volunteering habits?
2. What reasons for volunteering did teens most frequently cite, as stated by Independent Sector?
3. In the author's view, how can school courses increase teen volunteering?

Excerpted from *America's Teenage Volunteers: Civic Participation Begins Early in Life*, edited by Matthew Hamilton and Afshan Hussain (Washington, DC: Independent Sector, 1999). Copyright © 1999 by Independent Sector. Reprinted with permission.

A sk the average adult to use three or four words to describe the American teenager and chances are great that the word "volunteer" would not be mentioned. Yet more than half of America's teens reported volunteering in 1995.

Teens who volunteer increase their knowledge of the world and the problems that face it. Volunteering affords teens both an opportunity to shape their communities and to receive lifelong personal benefits. Furthermore, formal and informal volunteer experiences during teen years increase the possibility of continued volunteering in adulthood. Teen volunteering provides positive experiences for youth, benefits society, and establishes a foundation for lifelong civic duty.

Building the Habit of Volunteering

Several factors appear to encourage volunteering as a habit: the age when young people start to volunteer; the exposure to volunteering opportunities through religious, educational, or other institutions; and the role of positive self-images and role models.

Age
- Volunteering is an activity most likely to be cultivated early in childhood and during early teenage years. Adults who report volunteering in their youth are twice as likely to volunteer as adults. More than one out of three of all teenagers, six out of ten volunteers, started volunteering by the age of 14.

Opportunity
- Teens were nearly four times more likely to volunteer if they were asked than if they were not. Of the teens who reported being asked to volunteer, 93% actually did. Of the 49% who were not asked only 24% reported having volunteered. Non-whites were far less likely to be asked to volunteer than their white counterparts.
- Eighty percent of teens reported volunteering if, as young children, they did some volunteer work, were active in religious organizations, or were involved in student government.

Institutional Influence
- Teens reported first getting involved at either school (50%) and/or religious institutions (53%). Eight out of

ten volunteers were asked by someone at these institutions to volunteer.

- Religious institutions appear to influence teens in building not only habits of volunteering, but also of giving. Seven out of ten teen volunteers and nearly three out of four teen contributors attended religious services weekly or once or twice a month.
- Formal course work in community service appears to serve an important function in encouraging volunteering. Although teens reported preferring the choice to engage in service activities voluntarily, most did not react negatively to programs requiring service.
- Teens who took a course requiring community service emphasized the importance of the societal and personal benefits received from volunteering more frequently than those teen volunteers who did not take such a course.
- A greater percentage of teens volunteered who attended schools which offer a course requiring community service—even if they did not take the course.

Positive Self-Images

- Over 70% of teens reported that volunteering is important because it gives them a new perspective, allows them to do something for a cause that is important, and is an important activity to the people they respect.
- Teens had a higher volunteer rate than average (at least 70% compared with 59%) if they believed that social problems like poverty and hopelessness can be overcome through volunteer efforts; felt a moral duty to help people who suffer; or believed that it is within their power to do things that improve the welfare of others.

Positive Role Models

- Teens who reported having positive role models were nearly twice as likely to volunteer as those who did not.

Volunteering is an opportunity for teens to both give and receive. Teenagers reported both societal and personal benefits from their volunteering. Teens also identified volunteering as an opportunity to fulfill their own need to give.

- As a result of their volunteer efforts, teens reported doing better in school or improving grades, developing

Family Volunteering

How families benefit from volunteering

- They gain a shared sense of accomplishment and satisfaction from giving back to the community
- They can discuss service and community issues and get to know each other better
- Volunteering creates positive role models for children and youth
- Volunteering can help families learn about their own community and social issues that affect it
- Volunteering promotes civic responsibility and enhances a family's sense of community
- Volunteering builds the self-confidence of family members
- Volunteering improves communication and support skills in the family and in the community
- Volunteering creates a history of family memories
- Volunteers meet people of diverse cultural and economic backgrounds
- Volunteers have an opportunity to share time and talents
- Volunteering experiences carry over into other parts of volunteers' lives
- Giving to others places a volunteer's own problems in perspective

---

new career goals, and learning about career options.
- Other significant benefits included: learning how to respect others; learning to be helpful and kind; understanding people who are different from themselves; finding opportunities to develop leadership skills; becoming more patient; and understanding the qualities of good citizenship.
- The reasons teens cited most frequently for volunteering were: feeling compassion towards people in need; doing something for a cause that was important to them; and believing that if they helped others, others would help them.
- Two out of three respondents cited the following major reasons for being kind and caring: "Society is better off when we care for each other," and, "It makes me feel good about myself when I care for others."

- Volunteering forges special bonds between family members
- Volunteering helps children and teenagers to relate to other generations
- Volunteering gives families an opportunity to be together
- Volunteering makes families feel valued
- Families can make new social contacts
- Volunteer work can show families new ways to solve their own conflicts
- Volunteer work gives families a sense of purpose or belonging
- Families can participate together in special events (e.g., walk-a-thons) without having to leave the kids behind
- Volunteering develops family pride
- Volunteering can relieve isolation (for newcomers, new parents, etc.)

The institution of the family has long been seen as a basic building block of our communities. We all have our share of problems, but in the end, it is the family that shapes our children, and thus our society.

Kristen Porritt, *Family Volunteering: The Ties That Bind*, 1995.

- From their volunteer experience teens reported that they learned how to solve community problems; understood more about good citizenship; became more aware of programs in their communities; and learned more about how government and voluntary organizations work.

Teen volunteering impacts the young person and society. Volunteering promotes helping others, affords opportunities to achieve success as a member of a group that serves the community, broadens one's experience, and increases a teen's understanding of self and society.

What Can You Do?

- Ask young people to volunteer, particularly people of color. Minorities volunteer at about the same rate as whites when asked to do so.
- Provide young people with opportunities to take courses

and reflect on their community service. These courses help put the significance of community service and its benefits to society and individuals in context. Without this interaction and reflection young people are forced to discover the benefits they can both gain and give on their own.

- Encourage children to get involved in volunteering and/or civic participation at an early age. Volunteering when young creates lifelong adult givers and volunteers.
- Help young people develop positive self-images that encourage helping others, promote compassion for those in need, and instill a feeling that one can enact positive change in his or her community.
- Ensure that young people have positive role models.
- Increase opportunities for young people to volunteer in youth organizations, religious organizations, student governments and schools. Break down barriers to participation such as the lack of transportation or training.

Periodical Bibliography

The following articles have been selected to supplement the diverse views presented in this chapter.

American Legion	"Making Sense of the Senseless," July 1999.
Ulrich Boser	"The Unsparing Rod," *U.S. News & World Report*, June 18, 2001.
Joan Braune	"Children in the American Gulag," *Reclaiming Children and Youth*, Summer 2001.
David Broder	"A Service to the Country," *Washington Post*, October 7, 2001.
William L. Hamilton	"How Suburban Design Is Failing American Teenagers," *New York Times*, May 6, 1999.
Melissa Healy	"Zeal to Rein in Teens Grows, as Does Backlash," *Los Angeles Times*, July 3, 1999.
John McCain	"Putting the National in National Service," *Washington Monthly*, October 2001.
Sean Paige	"Is Something Rotten at the Entitlement Corps?" *Insight on the News*, December 14, 1998.
Janet Reno	"Taking America Back for Our Children," *Crime and Delinquency*, January 1998.
Sara Rimer	"Parents of Troubled Youths Are Seeking Help at Any Cost," *New York Times*, September 10, 2001.
James Taranto	"Zero Tolerance Makes Zero Sense," *Wall Street Journal*, May 18, 2001.
Emily Wax	"Rethinking Suspended Education; Instead of Just Going Home, Punished Students Get Classes, Counseling," *Washington Post*, January 12, 2002.
Ross Werland	"Parents Say Spying on Kids Is Worth It If It Keeps Them Out of Trouble," *San Diego Union-Tribune*, May 15, 1999.
Ray Wisher	"The Army Knows Best," *American Enterprise*, September 1999.

For Further Discussion

Chapter 1

1. Mike Males contends that emphasizing the negative influence of popular culture on youths diverts attention from the detrimental effects of socioeconomic factors such as poverty and family dysfunction. In contrast, William J. Bennett maintains that popular culture harms youths by glamorizing violence and antisocial behavior. In your opinion, do William J. Bennett's claims against popular culture divert attention from youths' socioeconomic problems? Explain your answer.

2. Michael T. Ungar asserts that peer pressure is a myth used by adults to explain the negative behaviors of youths. In your view, does Kathiann M. Kowalski make use of this myth to explain youth behavior? Use examples from the viewpoints to develop your answer.

3. Do you agree with Thomas Sowell's argument that programs in schools such as drug prevention and sex education undermine parental influence? Why or why not?

Chapter 2

1. Mike Males insists that focusing on youth substance abuse hinders the drug war because it ignores the greater prevalence of substance abuse among adults. Do you agree or disagree with the author? Use examples from the viewpoints to support your answer.

2. The National Campaign to Prevent Teen Pregnancy claims that the future economic prospects of teenagers sharply decline if they have a baby, since the mother is less likely to complete high school. However, Maggie Gallagher claims that the economic situation of teenagers with children can be significantly enhanced through marriage. In your opinion, should teenage couples expecting a child get married for its economic benefits? Why or why not?

3. Sue Smith-Heavenrich argues that schools should have less tolerance for bullying because such behavior can lead some of its victims to commit acts of violence and suicide. On the other hand, Benjamin Soskis contends that broadening antibullying policies in schools would be counterproductive because such policies demonize normal adolescent behavior. In your opinion, who makes the more compelling argument? Use examples from the viewpoints to explain your response.

Chapter 3

1. Judging from their survey, the Barna Research Group contends that youth interest in religion has been declining. In your view, is this a negative trend? Explain your answer.

2. The Alliance for Better Campaigns asserts that the media's failure to increase youths' awareness of current issues has resulted in their general disinterest in politics. In your opinion, is it the media's responsibility to encourage youths' interest in politics? Why or why not?

3. David J. Cherrington and J. Owen Cherrington claim that most youths do not have positive work ethics because today's economic and social prosperity shields them from hardship. Do you believe their claim has any validity? Explain your answer.

Chapter 4

1. In your opinion, do Louise B. Silverstein and Carl F. Auerbach successfully counter David Popenoe's claim that fathering provides intellectual and behavioral benefits that mothering cannot? Use examples from the viewpoints to develop your answer.

2. Kevin Ryan and Karen Bohlin contend that ethical values should be taught in the classroom. List three ethical values you think should be taught in schools and explain why you give these values particular importance.

Organizations to Contact

The editors have compiled the following list of organizations concerned with the issues debated in this book. The descriptions are derived from materials provided by the organizations. All have publications or information available for interested readers. The list was compiled on the date of publication of the present volume; the information provided here may change. Be aware that many organizations take several weeks or longer to respond to inquiries, so allow as much time as possible.

Advocates for Youth
1025 Vermont Ave. NW, Suite 200, Washington, DC 20005
(202) 347-5700 • fax: (202) 347-2263
e-mail: info@advocatesforyouth.org
website: www.advocatesforyouth.org

Advocates for Youth is the only national organization focusing solely on pregnancy and HIV prevention among young people. It provides information, education, and advocacy to youth-serving agencies and professionals, policymakers, and the media. Among the organization's numerous publications are the brochures *Advice from Teens on Buying Condoms* and *Spread the Word—Not the Virus* and the pamphlet *How to Prevent Date Rape: Teen Tips*.

American Civil Liberties Union (ACLU)
125 Broad St., 18th Floor, New York, NY 10004
(212) 549-2500 • fax (212) 549-2646
e-mail: aclu@aclu.org • website: www.aclu.org

The ACLU is a national organization that works to defend Americans' civil rights as guaranteed by the U.S. Constitution. It works to protect students' rights regarding issues such as freedom of speech and drug testing. The ACLU's numerous publications include the briefing papers "Reproductive Freedom: The Rights of Minors," "Point of View: School Uniforms," and "Equality in Education."

Family Research Council (FRC)
801 G St. NW, Washington, DC 20001
(202) 393-2100
website: www.frc.org

FRC seeks to promote and protect the interests of the traditional family. It focuses on issues such as parental autonomy and responsibility, community supports for single parents, and adolescent pregnancy. Among the council's numerous publications are the monthly *Drug Facts* and the biweekly *Culture Facts*.

The Jason Foundation, Inc.
116 Maple Row Blvd., Suite C, Hendersonville, TN 37075
(888) 881-2323 • fax: (615) 264-0188
website: www.jasonfoundation.com

Begun in 1997, The Jason Foundation helps educate students, parents, teachers, and others who work with young people about youth suicide. It offers special seminars and targeted programs designed to build awareness and provide life-saving information. All seminars and materials are free of charge.

Job Corps
(800) 733-JOBS
e-mail: webmaster@jcdc.jobcorp.org
website: http://jobcorps.doleta.gov

Job Corps is a division of the Employment and Training Administration at the U.S. Department of Labor and was founded in 1964. It provides America's disadvantaged youth with training designed to prepare them for the workplace. It also supplies employers with trained employees and communities with added resources and support. More than 120 Job Corps campuses exist nationwide, including those in the District of Columbia and Puerto Rico.

National Campaign to Prevent Teen Pregnancy
21 M St. NW, Suite 300, Washington, DC 20037
(202) 261-5655
website: www.teenpregnancy.org

The mission of the National Campaign is to reduce teenage pregnancy by promoting values and activities that are consistent with a pregnancy-free adolescence. The campaign's goal is to reduce the pregnancy rate among teenage girls by one-third by the year 2005. The campaign publishes pamphlets, brochures, and opinion polls that include *No Easy Answers: Research Findings on Programs to Reduce Teen Pregnancy*, *Not Just for Girls: Involving Boys and Men in Teen Pregnancy Prevention*, and *Public Opinion Polls and Teen Pregnancy*.

National School Safety Center (NSSC)
141 Duesenberg Dr., Suite 11, Westlake Village, CA 91362
(805) 373-9977 • fax: (805) 373-9277
e-mail: info@nssc1.org • website: www.nssc1.org

The NSSC is a research organization that studies school crime and violence, including hate crimes. The center believes that teacher training is an effective means of reducing these problems. Its publications include the book *Gangs in Schools: Breaking Up Is Hard to*

Do and the *School Safety Update* newsletter, which is published nine times a year.

Office of Juvenile Justice and Delinquency Prevention (OJJDP)
U.S. Department of Justice
810 Seventh St. NW, Washington, DC 20531
(202) 307-5911 • fax: (202) 307-2093
e-mail: Askjj@ncjrs.org • website: http://ojjdp.ncjrs.org

OJJDP provides national leadership and resources to prevent and respond to juvenile delinquency. It supports community efforts to develop effective programs and improve the juvenile justice system. Publications available at its website include "School House Hype: School Shootings and the Real Risks Kids Face in America" and "Kids and Guns: From Playground to Battlegrounds."

OutProud, The National Coalition for Gay, Lesbian, Bisexual & Transgender Youth
369 Third St., Suite B-362
San Rafael, CA 94901-3581
e-mail: info@outproud.org • website: www.outproud.org

OutProud aims to help homosexual youth become happy, successful, confident, and vital gay, lesbian, and bisexual adults. The coalition provides outreach and support to gay teens just coming to terms with their sexual orientation and to those contemplating coming out. On its website, OutProud offers brochures on a variety of gay youth programs and resources and forums for gay youth to correspond with one another.

Society for Adolescent Medicine (SAM)
1916 NW Copper Oaks Circle, Blue Springs, MO 64015
(816) 224-8010
website: www.adolescenthealth.org

SAM is a multidisciplinary organization of professionals committed to improving the physical and psychosocial health and well-being of all adolescents. It helps plan and coordinate national and international professional education programs on adolescent health. Its publications include the monthly *Journal of Adolescent Health* and the quarterly *SAM Newsletter*.

Teen Advice.Net
http://teenadvice.studentcenter.org

Teen Advice.Net offers students and teens expert and peer advice about health, body image, relationships, sexuality, gender issues, and other teen concerns. The web page was created by The Student Center, a web community for college students, high school students, and teenagers.

Teen Advice Online (TAO)
www.teenadviceonline.org

TAO's teen counselors from around the world offer advice for teens on health, fitness, dieting, body image, family, school, substance abuse, dating, sex and sexuality, gender issues, and relationships. Teens can submit questions to the counselors or read about similar problems in the archives.

Teen-Aid
723 E. Jackson Ave., Spokane, WA 99207
(509) 482-2868
e-mail: teenaid@teen-aid.org • website: www.teen-aid.org

Teen-Aid is an international organization that promotes traditional family values and sexual morality. It publishes a public school sex education curriculum, *Sexuality, Commitment and Family*, stressing sexual abstinence before marriage.

The Unusual Suspects
PO Box 360975
Los Angeles, CA 90036-1475
(323) 634-0383 • fax: (323) 634-0384
e-mail: Unusuallh@aol.com
website: www.theunusualsuspects.org

Created after the 1993 Los Angeles riots, The Unusual Suspects Theatre Company was formed to bring theater arts to at-risk youth. Through improvisation and writing exercises, professionals in the arts participating in The Unusual Suspects programs work to help young people create original theater and to foster pride, self-confidence, and racial tolerance.

WholeFamily
www.wholefamily.com

This source is designed for both parents and teens. The site's advice columnist, Liz, answers questions about body image, dieting, fitness, teen sex, drugs, drinking, and pregnancy, while online articles discuss other issues such as divorce, relationships, and health.

Young Life (YL)
PO Box 520, Colorado Springs, CO
(719) 381-1800
website: www.younglife.org

YL is a Christian ministry that reaches out to junior high and high school aged kids. The nonprofit organization currently operates in communities across the United States, and in about fifty three other countries. YL seeks to become a positive influence in youths' lives, connecting with them at high school sporting events, concerts, plays, malls, and fast-food restaurants.

Youth Crime Watch of America (YCWA)
9300 S. Dadeland Blvd., Suite 100, Miami, FL 33156
(305) 670-2409 • fax: (305) 670-3805
e-mail: ycwa@ycwa.org • website: www.ycwa.org

YCWA is a nonprofit, student-led organization that promotes crime and drug prevention programs in communities and schools throughout the United States. Member-students at the elementary and secondary level help raise others' awareness concerning alcohol and drug abuse, crime, gangs, guns, and the importance of staying in school. Strategies include organizing student assemblies and patrols, conducting workshops, and challenging students to become personally involved in preventing crime and violence. YCWA publishes the quarterly newsletter *National Newswatch* and the *Community Based Youth Crime Watch Program Handbook*.

Bibliography of Books

Robert Agnew — *Juvenile Delinquency: Causes and Control*. Los Angeles: Roxbury, 2000.

Joe Ambrose — *Moshpit: The Violent World of Mosh Pit Culture*. London: Omnibus, 2001.

Mark Aronson — *Exploding the Myths: The Truth About Teenagers and Reading*. Lanham, MD: Scarecrow Press, 2001.

George Barna — *Generation Next: What You Need to Know About Today's Youth*. Ventura, CA: Regal Books, 1997.

Douglas Besharov, ed. — *America's Disconnected Youth: Toward a Preventative Strategy*. Washington, DC: CWLA Press, 1999.

Randy Blazak and Wayne S. Wooden — *Renegade Kids, Suburban Outlaws: From Youth Culture to Delinquency*. Florence, KY: Wadsworth, 2000.

Kathryn Borman and Barbara Schneider, eds. — *The Adolescent Years: Social Influences and Educational Challenges*. Chicago: University of Chicago Press, 1998.

James E. Côté and Anton L. Allahar — *Generation on Hold: Coming of Age in the Late Twentieth Century*. New York: New York University Press, 1996.

Mihaly Csikszentmihalyi and Barbara Schneider — *Becoming Adult: How Teenagers Prepare for the World of Work*. New York: Basic Books, 2000.

Linnea A. Due — *Joining the Tribe: Growing Up Gay and Lesbian in the '90s*. New York: Anchor Books, 1995.

David Elkind — *All Grown Up and No Place to Go: Teenagers in Crisis*. Reading, MA: Addison-Wesley, 1998.

Delbert S. Elliot, Beatrix A. Hamburg, and Kirk R. Williams — *Violence in American Schools*. Cambridge, UK: Cambridge University Press, 1998.

Jonathan Epstein, ed. — *Youth Culture: Identity in a Postmodern World*. Williston, VT: Blackwell Publishing, 1998.

Ronald B. Flowers — *Runaway Kids and Teenage Prostitution: America's Lost, Abandoned, and Sexually Exploited Children*. Westport, CT: Greenwood Press, 2001.

Henry A. Giroux — *Channel Surfing: Racism, the Media, and the Destruction of Today's Youth*. Torrance, CA: Griffin Trade Paperbacks, 1998.

Henry A. Giroux

Stealing Innocence: Youth, Corporate Power, and the Politics of Culture. New York: St. Martin's Press, 2000.

Kathleen A. Hempelman

Teen Legal Rights. Westport, CT: Greenwood Press, 2000.

Alan Henderson, Sally Champlin, and William Evashwick, eds.

Promoting Teen Health: Linking Schools, Health Organizations, and Community. Thousand Oaks, CA: Sage, 1998.

Patricia Hershch

A Tribe Apart: A Journey into the Heart of American Adolescence. New York: Ballantine, 1999.

Thomas Hine

The Rise and Fall of the American Teenager. New York: Bard, 1999.

Mary Motley Kalergis

Seen and Heard: Teenagers Talk About Their Lives. New York: Stewart, Tobori & Chang, 1998.

Richard M. Lerner and Daniel F. Perkins, eds.

Social Interactions in Adolescence and Promoting Positive Social Contributions of Youth. New York: Garland, 1999.

Roger J.R. Levesque

Adolescents, Sex, and the Law: Preparing Adolescents for Responsible Citizenship. Washington, DC: American Psychological Association, 2000.

Mike Males

Framing Youth: Ten Myths About the Next Generation. Monroe, ME: Common Courage Press, 1999.

Mike Males

The Scapegoat Generation: America's War on Adolescents. Monroe, ME: Common Courage Press, 1996.

Jeffrey P. Moran

Teaching Sex: The Shaping of Adolescence in the Twentieth Century. Cambridge, MA: Harvard University Press, 2000.

Wilda Webber Morris

Stop the Violence: Educating Ourselves to Protect Our Youth. Valley Forge, PA: Judson Press, 2001.

Lynn E. Ponton

The Sex Lives of Teenagers: Revealing the Secret World of Adolescent Boys and Girls. New York: Plume, 2001.

Jessica Portner

One in Thirteen: The Silent Epidemic of Teen Suicide. Beltsville, MD. Robins Lane Press, 2001.

Thom S. Rainer

The Bridger Generation: America's Second Largest Generation, What They Believe, How to Reach Them. Nashville, TN: Broadman & Holman, 1997.

Paul R. Robbins

Adolescent Suicide. Jefferson, NC: McFarland & Co., 1998.

Sarah Shandler   *Ophelia Speaks: Adolescent Girls Write About Their Search for Self.* New York: HarperPerennial, 1999.

Ron Taffel and   *The Second Family: Reckoning with Adolescent
Melinda Blau   Power.* New York: St. Martin's Press, 2001.

Niobe Way   *Everyday Courage: The Lives and Stories of Urban Teens.* New York: New York University Press, 1998.

Wendy Murray Zoba   *Generation 2K: What Parents and Others Need to Know About the Millenials.* Downers Grove, IL: Intervarsity Press, 1999.

Index

abortion
  teenage, decline in, 29
Adler, Jerry, 14, 17
adolescents
  are politically apathetic, 145–48
    con, 140–44
    reasons for, 146–47
  are spoiled and lack work ethic,
    156–57, 158–59
    con, 151
  at-risk
    approaches to helping, 184–86
    community schools programs for,
      186
    Job Corps and, 162
    juvenile justice programs for,
      187–88
    peer pressure among, 48–50
  church-based involvement among,
    138
  developmental stages of power,
    47–48
  growth in population of, will fuel
    future crime wave, 173
  health risks of pregnancy in, 78
  improvements in conduct of, 29–30
  involvement in missionary work
    among, 129–34
  lack knowledge and basic skills,
    158–59
    con, 150–51
  most hold Christian values, 127–34
    con, 135–39
  normal problems of, 32
  principles for developing work values
    of, 159
  qualities brought to workplace by,
    152–53
  socialization of, 155
African Americans
  young male, firearm suicides among,
    97
Albores, Ariel, 36
alcohol
  availability of, 73
  use of, among teens, 69
    is decreasing, 74
    is increasing, 70
  see also drinking, binge
Alliance for Better Campaigns, 145
*Angry Young Men: How Parents,
  Teachers, and Counselors Can Help Bad
  Boys Become Good Men* (Kipnis), 16
Ashcroft, John, 113
Atlantic Monthly (magazine), 25

Auerbach, Carl F., 175
automobile accidents
  teen deaths from, 63

Badagliacco, Joanna, 125
Barna, George, 128, 139
Barna Research Group, 125, 135
Barnes, Seth, 128
Barone, Frank, 112
Bass, Jay, 16
Bennett, Stephen E., 147
Bennett, William J., 19, 29
Benton, Keith G., 100
births, out-of-wedlock
  prevalence of, 85, 101, 165
  to teenage mothers, 80
Black, Nathan, 14
Blum, William, 53, 56
Bohlin, Karen, 190
Bornstein, Robert, 36
Bratt, Marguerite Stevenson, 85
Bronfenbrenner, Urie, 86
Brown, B.B., 43
Bruen, Brett, 141–42
*Building Character in Schools: Practical
  Ways to Bring Moral Instruction to Life*
  (Ryan and Bohlin), 190
bullies
  characteristics of, 108–109
  ways parents can help, 111–12
bullying
  connection with school violence,
    116–17
  defining, problems with, 118–20
  efforts to combat, risks of, 120–21
  prevalence of, 116
  school intervention in, 112–14
  victims of
    characteristics of, 109–10
    how parents can help, 110–11
  among youths
    extent of, is exaggerated, 115–22
    con, 106–14

Carnegie Corporation, 32
Champion, H.R., 95
Change the Climate, 73
character education
  addition to curricula, barriers to,
    193–94
  should build on students' existing
    values, 194
  survey on, 191–93
Cherrington, David J., 154
Cherrington, J. Owen, 154